KEYS TO INVESTING IN GOVERNMENT SECURITIES

Jay Goldinger

Investment Counselor, Capital Insight
Beverly Hills, California

BARRON'S

New York • London • Toronto • Sydney

All inquiries should be addressed to:
Barron's Educational Series, Inc.
250 Wireless Boulevard
Hauppauge, New York 11788

Library of Congress Catalog Card No. 90-20302

International Standard Book No. 0-8120-4485-1

Library of Congress Cataloging in Publication Data
Goldinger, Jay.
    Keys to investing in government securities / Jay Goldinger.
        p.   cm.—(Barron's business keys)
    Includes index.
    ISBN 0-8120-4485-1
    1. Government securities—United States.   2. Investments.
I. Title.   II. Series.
    HG4936.G65   1991
332.63′232—dc20   90-20302
                                                                          CIP

PRINTED IN THE UNITED STATES OF AMERICA
1234   5500   987654321

CONTENTS

INTRODUCTION

During a 15-year career as a bond broker investing my clients' money and my own in the U.S. Government securities markets here and around the world, I've learned the hard way how to win and lose. And as a member of the senior team—most recently with Cantor, Fitzgerald & Company, quite possibly the nation's largest U.S. Government bond brokerage, and now as an investment counselor with Capital Insight Brokerage—I've watched how Wall Street sells the concept of treasuries to Main Street.

It doesn't.

For the most part, *institutional investors*—banks, pensions and other retirement funds, mutual funds and other investment firms—dominate the U.S. Treasury markets. They know, from a credit-risk standpoint, that treasuries are the safest investment in the world; they have no default worries. From a market-risk standpoint, such investors have access to the best information and the finest money management minds to limit their losses and produce profits—in sick or in healthy economic times.

What about Main Street? Most individual investors generally stick with treasury bills, short-term and safe, and rarely venture beyond. No surprise here. The U.S. Government bond market, despite its size, strength, and safety record, is about as familiar to investors as the far side of the moon. The fact is that stockbrokers feel comfortable selling stocks and packaged investments with more action and bigger commissions. Bond brokers are a rare breed; the best ones who have mastered the market are investing their own money and work with a limited number of knowledgeable clients. They don't peddle, cold call, or dial for dollars.

And that's exactly why I wrote this book. I wanted to make you, the reader, street savvy while giving you a guided tour of what is probably the most fascinating of all investments once you understand how the U.S. Government bond market really works. I wanted to arm you with the information you need to make a profit on treasuries regardless of the economic climate.

We'll start with the basics, and you'll see that the bond market is very different from the stock market. The bond market is almost totally driven by changes in interest rates. Remember this fundamental truth: Interest rates go up; treasury bill, note, and bond yields go up; but prices go down. Interest rates go down, yields go down, but prices go up. No earnings per share to watch, industry health to worry about, or consumer buying habits to track. Those are fundamentals of the stock market, not the bond market.

With treasuries, you must keep plugged in on a more macroeconomic scale, and I'll show you how to do it. Monitoring the economic statistics that are issued regularly out of Washington, D.C., helps you gauge inflationary pressures. Watching the Federal Reserve and anticipating what it is about to do helps you keep in perspective how the rest of the world *thinks* those policymakers will be acting. This is one case where it pays, literally, to be an informed investor.

Your reasons for wanting to add treasuries to your portfolio may vary. You may simply want regular monthly income. You may want to protect and build your capital. Or you may want to venture out a bit on the risk/reward spectrum. Whether you invest through mutual funds or with a seasoned broker (and be sure to find one who is a winner investing his or her own money), you cannot exist in an informational vacuum. You need an edge.

I wrote this book for one reason: to give you that edge.

Jay Goldinger

1

A TOUR OF THE FEDERAL RESERVE

The second most powerful and influential person in the United States after the president is not the vice president, not the chairman of the New York Stock Exchange and not the chief justice of the Supreme Court. It is the chairman of the Board of Governors of the Federal Reserve. Apart from presidential pronouncements on tax policy, the Fed chairman's decisions have the single greatest impact on the economy—at home and abroad and on investors in U.S. Government securities.

The chairman of the Federal Reserve controls the twin faucets of cash and credit that feed the U.S. monetary system. In truth, he largely controls short-term interest rates, capital borrowing, and corporate and economic growth.

The Fed chairman, although appointed by the president for a four-year term, answers to no one. He is—and should be—free of political pressure, although that is not always the case. The White House and Congress often make their feelings known, subtly, of course. Nevertheless, as the architect of U.S. monetary policy, he has the delicate yet demanding task of regulating the flow of credit to promote orderly, sustained economic expansion without triggering inflation.

Now what does this mean in plain English? Simply that you should understand how the Fed works and keep an eye on what it does. As an investor, it affects your bottom line.

Established by Congress in 1913 as a "central bank" for the United States so commercial banks could meet demands by farmers for cash and currency to plant and harvest crops, the Fed today is a network of 12 Federal Reserve Banks, plus branches.

The heart and soul of the Federal Reserve is the Federal Open Market Committee (FOMC). Membership is comprised of the seven-person Federal Reserve Board of Governors plus the presidents of 12 Federal Reserve Banks. The FOMC, which meets eight times a year to set and fine tune monetary policy, has two goals: first, curb inflation by maintaining the extremely delicate balance between cash, credit and debt and, second, promote a healthy long-term economic environment by preserving the value of the dollar.

How does the Fed adjust monetary policy to achieve these twin goals? Mainly by controlling the cash and credit faucets through buying or selling U.S. Government securities. This, in turn, builds or reduces bank reserves, as the economy expands or contracts. It also sets targets for bank reserves, percentage parameters for money supply growth, a desired "range" for Fed funds interest rates, and a total figure for non-financial debt.

As Joseph Coyne, chief spokesperson for the Federal Reserve puts it in summing up the Fed's broad objectives, "Keeping inflation under control is crucial for sustained long-term economic growth. Over the years we've learned that inflation causes recessions, and too much money causes inflation."

Think of the Fed's Federal Open Market Committee as the economy's accelerator or its brake pedal. For example, when members of the FOMC think the economy is slowing down, they can press down on the accelerator—pump cash into circulation—by going into the marketplace and buying treasury bills, notes or bonds.

If the FOMC feels the economy is overheating and inflation will make existing dollars worth less, it will put on the brakes by selling treasury securities it owns into the marketplace, thus removing money from circulation.

Whose foot is actually on the gas and brake pedals? It is a battery of people who work on what is called the Open Market Desk. If the Federal Open Market Committee is indeed the heart and soul of the Federal Reserve, the Open Market Desk is the nerve center. Tucked away on the eighth floor of the Federal Reserve Bank of New York, the "Desk" carries out, on a daily basis, the FOMC's monetary policy directives.

Every day at precisely 11:40 A.M. Eastern Time, "Fed-watchers" around the world, economists and professional investors, have their eyes and ears trained on the Open Market Desk. That's when the Fed's "daily operations" are executed, adding or draining cash—actually bank reserves—to (or from) the economy to keep the country's monetary policy on track for the next 24 hours. Unlike Congress, which has galleries where you can watch the action, the Open Market Desk conducts its operations in virtual secrecy. Many Fed employees themselves have never been in the busy room on the eighth floor.

2

BANK RESERVES: HOW THE FED MOVES THE MARKET

What makes the Open Market Desk the "single most powerful financial decision-making venue in the world"? The answer goes back to the roots of the commercial banking system.

By federal law, banks and all depository institutions—mutual savings banks, savings and loans, credit unions—must meet minimum reserve requirements. For every deposit on its books, a bank must set aside 12 percent of the dollar amount as a reserve. This can be stored as either cash in its own vault or as readily liquid securities placed in a non-interest-bearing account at one of the 12 regional branches of the Federal Reserve Bank.

Think of these bank reserve accounts as being the bank's own checking account, with the Fed having sole depository or check-writing privileges. (Banks cannot touch the cash reserves stored in their vaults, either.) These reserve accounts perform the internal functions of check cashing. For example, when your bank accepts your check drawn on another bank, the check is cleared by electronically crediting or debiting your bank's reserve account and debiting or crediting the reserve account at the bank on which your check was drawn on.

Historically, the Fed's reserve requirements have been thought of primarily as the best way to maintain a bank's liquidity so that the institution would have the cash to meet a customer's withdrawal or to cover any losses of funds. Recently, however, the Federal Deposit Insurance

Corporation and the Fed's role as the lender of last resort have removed the liquidity burdens from bank reserves. Today, bank reserves are generally considered to be a monetary policy tool that can be adjusted and fine-tuned by the Open Market Desk.

Here's how that is accomplished. When the Fed wants to adjust monetary policy, it either buys or sells U.S. Government securities. To ease credit and promote economic growth, the Fed buys very short-term securities in the open market from one of its primary dealers. It pays for the securities by electronically crediting the bank with Federal Reserve notes, which are the equivalent of cash. With this new influx of money, the bank must set aside approximately 12 percent of it as reserves. The deposit, minus the reserves, gives the bank more money to lend out. Hence, the Fed has pumped more money into the system, credit is eased, and theoretically, economic expansion is promoted.

Now, to tighten credit and slow economic growth, the Fed does the reverse. It sells U.S. Government securities from its own inventory to a primary dealer and takes the money it receives out of circulation and out of the monetary system. At the same time, when the primary dealer pays for the securities it has just bought from the Fed, the bank reserves set aside for that dealer's money are wiped out. The process is called "draining the reserves." And with reduced deposits and fewer reserves, the bank doesn't have as much money to lend. With fewer funds to loan out, the bank can put its money out at a higher interest rate; some borrowers will resist and economic growth is discouraged. Thus the Fed has achieved its goal of reducing the money supply and tightening credit, a tactic used to combat inflation. It also controls the currency or cash in circulation. (See Key 1 on money supply.)

Suppose that banks need additional reserves to meet higher loan demand. They are not forced to rely on the Fed to shore up these reserves when they run short. They can bypass the Fed and borrow money overnight, or for longer periods, from other banks with excess reserves.

This is called the Federal Funds market and the rate of interest, called the Federal Funds Rate, is set by the institutions but influenced by the Fed. The Fed Funds Rate is a critical credit barometer because almost all short-term rates—and yields—react to a change in the Fed Funds Rate.

On the other hand, long-term interest rates are primarily determined by inflationary expectations.

The Open Market Desk manager has a variety of tools at his disposal to influence monetary policy on a day-to-day basis. As an alternative to permanent sales or purchases of U.S. Government securities, to add to or drain bank reserves, a more common strategy is to use a "repurchase agreement," sometimes known as an "RP" or a "repo." This is a temporary purchase of government securities, usually for one day but it can be for as long as seven days.

For instance, if the Fed wants to create reserves, the Desk purchases government securities in the open market from a primary dealer or foreign central bank and agrees to sell them back to the institution the following day at the same rate plus interest.

The opposite strategy is a "matched sale," or what is sometimes called a "reverse repo." This is a tool used by the Fed to drain reserves and tighten the money supply. To execute a matched sale, the Open Market Desk sells U.S. Government securities to a primary dealer or a foreign central bank, agreeing to buy them back on a specific date, usually in one to seven days, at the same price.

The question you are probably asking yourself is this: "As a private investor, do I really have to be a daily 'Fedwatcher' to be successful?" Absolutely not. But you should pay attention to FOMC actions as they are reported in the press and keep on top of the monthly and quarterly announcements and pronouncements that come out of Washington, D.C.

Information, as much as you can get, gives you—above all—the edge you need to invest intelligently in U.S. Government securities.

3

PRIMARY DEALERS: UNCLE SAM'S BIGGEST AND BEST CUSTOMERS

When the U.S. Treasury needs money to run the country, it holds auctions and sells bills, notes, and bonds to the highest bidder. Private investors, of course, can buy directly from the Treasury. But the U.S. government's biggest customers, who buy an average of 80 to 90 percent of new federal debt at Treasury auctions, are called primary dealers.

Primary dealers are also called "market makers"— they maintain an inventory of treasury issues and can sell them into the market to break a logjam, that is, when everyone is a buyer and prices are rising.

On the flip side of that coin, primary dealers have the financial muscle to buy the excess treasuries when investors are selling. But they are not required to step in and stabilize the market; they must only quote a "bid" or "ask," and it doesn't have to be the lowest or highest. In short, primary dealers help the Federal Reserve—the nation's central bank—regulate the money supply.

Who are these primary dealers? They are 40 financial institutions worldwide—Merrill Lynch, Shearson Lehman, Goldman Sachs, Citibank, Security Pacific Bank—and include Japanese banks and brokerages such as Fuji Bank, Nikko Securities, Nomura Securities, and Daiwa.

Size alone does not qualify a financial institution for a primary dealership. But it helps. "You have to earn it," notes Edward S. Bradley, vice president of the training department of Salomon Brothers, the largest of all primary dealers.

7

To "earn" the primary dealer designation and, thus, the opportunity to bid on huge lots of treasuries at auction, a financial institution must be able to buy or finance enough treasuries to account for 1 percent of the total secondary, or resale, market. What does 1 percent translate into, dollarwise? The Fed says that number varies so sharply from week to week or month to month that it cannot accurately state what that represents in hard dollars. Some $100 billion in U.S. Treasury securities, on average, trade every day in the secondary market. However, the total public debt comprised of outstanding treasury bills, notes, and bonds and some federal financing securities stood at over $2 trillion late in 1990 and, unfortunately, is growing by the second.

While primary dealers are also brokerage firms that sell to the public, a small investor can go straight to the Federal Reserve Bank and buy direct from the Treasury at auction and not pay a fee or a commission. However, the price, theoretically, could be higher than purchasing from a bond broker at a brokerage firm that buys wholesale through a primary dealer.

Remember, the 40 primary dealers and other financial institutions that aspire to this designation do not simply warehouse treasuries as a favor to the U.S. government. They are continually buying and selling minimum $1 million lots of bills, bonds and notes, usually to and from each other, trying to earn a profit on every trade.

They also wholesale huge blocks of governments to pension funds, mutual funds, banks, and other institutions, and they fill the buy/sell orders of individual investors placed through the nation's 6,000 brokerage firms.

However, as an individual investor buying the U.S. Government securities individually rather than through a mutual fund, you should hope your personal broker does not have a cozy relationship with just one primary dealer. The U.S. government bond market is a global bazaar with at least 40 mercenary merchants all scrambling for the best profit. Just make sure someone is haggling hard on your behalf.

4

TREASURY BILLS: BETTER THAN CASH FOR THE CONSERVATIVE INVESTOR

The first treasury bill was sold in 1929—the year, co-incidentally, the stock market suffered its first major crash. That T-bill, however, was redeemed at maturity, on schedule, and in the six decades since, Uncle Sam has always paid off his IOUs.

That's exactly what a treasury bill is. The federal government borrows money weekly to keep its cash flowing—to meet its expenses while waiting to collect its income. And of all the IOUs issued, T-bills, backed by the full faith and credit of the U.S. Treasury, are the closest certificates there are to cash.

In fact, treasury bills can be even better than cash. They can be cashed out immediately, sometimes for more than 100 cents on the dollar (and sometimes for less). They are also remarkably flexible investments yielding a high, market rate of interest that can be purchased at a discount. There is no commission if you buy them directly from the government. Nor are there any custodial fees.

The yields on treasury bills are also tax-advantaged. Unlike other fixed income securities such as certificates of deposit, corporate bonds, or commercial paper, you pay no state or local taxes on the income earned or the price appreciation realized. Only federal taxes are assessed.

Indeed, treasury bills are probably the wisest choice

for investors who want absolutely no risk whatsoever and who can commit their cash for periods ranging from one week to one year. T-bills are also a smart place to park cash between investments. For instance, if you sell stocks or cash out of a retirement plan and you're looking for a cabin on the lake or a condo at the shore, T-bills are a smart place to put the proceeds, especially if interest rates are drifting downward. You get a yield floor—a minimum guaranteed yield or return—for at least three months, up to a year, while rates for a money market mutual fund fluctuate daily. On the other hand, if short-term interest rates are rising slowly, you can roll over T-bills rather than bank certificates of deposit as a conservative strategy and not worry about the price volatility that afflicts treasury notes and bonds with longer maturities.

But the hard fact is that too many investors ignore the benefits of T-bills and opt instead for certificates of deposit. This can be a big mistake. Here's why.

Investors and savers gravitate toward CDs at banks and savings and loans because, they say, they are federally insured. True, but only up to $100,000. And with the thrift industry and a small but startling number of banks scratching for profits, you have to wonder why one would choose a CD over a T-bill, which is also federally guaranteed and for a lot more than $100,000. In fact, there is no ceiling.

Aside from safety, certificates of deposit are *not* liquid, whereas treasury bills are. You can liquidate them at any time in the secondary market (see Key 5) without penalty. If you break a CD before maturity, there is a "substantial withdrawal penalty" that could cost you a hefty chunk of your interest.

The point is, as an investor, you never know when a great investment opportunity will present itself. People locked into a bank CD cannot get their money out easily to take advantage of a sound investment. With a T-bill, regardless of whether it was bought at a bank or brokerage, cash is a phone call away.

5

PURCHASING TREASURY BILLS

How are T-bills issued, bought, and sold? Basically, they come in three maturities: 13 weeks (or 91 days), 26 weeks (or 182 days), and 52 weeks (or 364 days). The minimum purchase is $10,000; $5,000 increments may be bought after that. Investors who purchase T-bills are loaning the Treasury at least $10,000 for three months, six months, or a year, and that money is repaid with interest. T-bills are auctioned weekly, usually on Monday (one-year T-bills are auctioned monthly on a Thursday), and the interest rate is set by market rates at the time and announced (but not set by) the Treasury.

A T-bill auction conjures up images of shouting out the price you'll pay as you would for a rare work of art or a prized Chateau Lafite Rothschild. It really isn't that adventurous. You can buy the T-bills directly from the government at no commission, or through a bank or brokerage firm that might charge you an administrative fee ranging from $25 to $60, depending on whether it is buying the bills at auction or through the secondary market. (Again, the secondary market is where previously issued T-bills are bought and sold daily.) If you hold the bills to maturity, you pay no selling commission.

However, if you sell the bonds through a brokerage firm before they mature, you'll pay another $25 to $60 fee or commission. The bottom line: Buy direct from the government, and save. The costliest approach is to use a treasury bill money market fund where the management fees can add unnecessary expenses that could chew up to a half percent off your investment. (On the other hand, T-bill money funds like Capital Preservation Fund do not require the $10,000 minimum investment that you

11

for a direct purchase, and a professional money manager is making the buy and sell decisions.)

The steps for buying direct from the government are relatively simple. You contact one of the branch offices of the Federal Reserve Bank or the Treasury Department's Bureau of Public Debt (see page 120 for addresses and phone numbers) and request a form for what's called a "noncompetitive tender." This means that when you put in your bid, the price you pay will be the average price of all T-bills sold that day at auction. (The "competitive bid," usually made by institutions buying over $1 million, is a stated yield the buyer is willing to accept, but individual investors aren't big enough buyers to be take-it-or-leave-it bidders.)

Submitting a tender automatically opens a Treasury Direct Account and gives you an account number used for subsequent purchases. It must be accompanied with full payment, either by a cashier's check, certified personal check, other maturing Treasury securities, or cash. When you buy through a Treasury Direct Account, you may also instruct the government to roll over the bills to the next maturity for up to two years. It's wiser, though, to watch the maturities and rates yourself because you may want a different option at the end of 12 months.

The rate you'll get on that Monday auction will be quoted in the paper the following day and expressed on a discount basis and possibly a coupon equivalent. For example, if 13-week T-bills were auctioned at 7.73 percent, the coupon equivalent or yield to maturity might be 7.99 percent. Because the price, also, is discounted, the $10,000 in T-bills would cost you $9,804.60.

You can sell T-bills before they mature in the highly liquid secondary market, but you need a broker to execute the transaction. In fact, most people don't realize they do not have to wait until the auction on Mondays to buy T-bills; an experienced broker can buy—or sell—a T-bill for you 24 hours a day, Monday through Friday (markets do not trade on weekends). However, depending on market conditions, you may lose some principal if you sell before maturity. Supply and demand sets the T-bill price in the secondary market, so check out the proceeds you'll collect before you cash out.

Treasury bills can go to work for you in other ways while they are maturing. Many commercial banks and brokerages will accept T-bills as collateral if you will allow them to mature and the financial institution knows it can get its hands on cash if it has to offset your loan. In fact, bankers making secured personal loans prefer T-bills over stocks as a collateral pledge because stocks generally are more volatile and banks must monitor them closely during the life of your loan. Brokerages will also take T-bills as collateral when you purchase bonds or equities on margin.

T-bill prices should be monitored, too. In your daily newspaper, there are three figures quoted, the first two indicating the price. The bid quote is a discounted yield that a dealer is willing to pay—the annualized discount from par or the face value. The ask quote is the same thing—the annualized discount from par that the seller is offering. But it's the third figure—the yield, or annualized rate of return, also called the "coupon equivalent"—that's the key figure. This is the actual rate of return you will receive by holding the bill to maturity, and this is the figure you should use when comparing yields of alternative investments. But, again, even that is not an absolute yield. Because T-bill quotes are taken at different times during the trading day, the yield shown in the newspaper does not necessarily reflect the last T-bill trade of the day.

To figure the actual worth of three- and six-month T-bills on a given day takes a little arithmetic. But just a little. You multiply the face value of the T-bill times the offer rate (expressed as a percentage) times the days remaining until maturity and divide the figure by 360 days. Subtract that figure from $10,000 and you find out the amount of cash you will have to put up to buy the bills. Again, the price appreciates as you get closer to maturity. An 8 percent six-month T-bill might be priced at $9,595 per $10,000 of face value. That same T-bill three months later—three months closer to maturity— might sell for $9,797.

Let's summarize and strategize. T-bills have amazing flexibility as an investment. Unlike certificates of deposit, where being locked into a maturity can cost you missed opportunities, T-bills can be turned into cash in a secondary market. T-bill yields are tax-advantaged. Comparing an 8 percent T-bill with an 8 percent CD is really no comparison. The T-bill's income and price appreciation are not subject to state or local taxes, and for a taxpayer in the 5 percent state income bracket, the T-bill's equivalent yield is 8.42 percent.

From a pure investment and financial planning strategy standpoint, T-bills make more sense than certificates of deposit as well. For example, many investors buy T-bills due April 15 to have the cash to pay their income tax obligation. But with a lot of demand for the same T-bill, the price soars, pushing the yield down. A smarter move is to buy a usually lower priced/higher yielding T-bill that matures after April 15, sell it before the IRS deadline day and put the proceeds into a money market mutual fund for four days. Chances are, you'll realize a profit, and you'll have the cash when you need it.

The trick with treasury bills, like any treasury security, is to know their strengths and shortcomings. Indeed, bankers, brokers, and other financial salespeople market CDs as convenient and safe. But for anyone willing to stack them up side by side with a treasury bill and weigh the pluses and minuses before they commit their capital, the choice is clear.

6

TREASURY NOTES: MORE RISK, MORE REWARD, STILL SAFE

Treasury notes are aimed at investors who are willing to lend money to the U.S. Government for more than a year so it can meet its financial obligations. Treasury notes are identical to treasury bills in two important ways: the principal—the money loaned or invested—is guaranteed to be redeemed 100 cents on the dollar if the notes are held to maturity, and the income earned by noteholders is not subject to state and local income taxes.

Indeed, there is absolutely no credit risk on these federal debt instruments, and the only tax obligation is to the U.S. Government.

But there are several crucial differences between treasury notes and treasury bills. First, T-notes have interest-bearing coupons attached that pay holders cash twice a year. With T-bills, the interest is factored into the discounted price and is paid at maturity.

Second, treasury notes are issued in maturities ranging from two to ten years, and the minimum purchase can be as low as $1,000. However, the last time the Treasury issued a $1,000 T-note with a maturity less than four years was in 1974. The $1,000 T-note today belongs on a wall, as a framed antique, not in an investment portfolio.

Usually, the Treasury auctions off T-notes in denominations of $5,000 increments, but they also come in $10,000, $100,000, and $1 million denominations. The auctions are held on a strangely staggered schedule. Two-year T-notes come out once a month. Three-year and ten-year notes are auctioned quarterly—on the first week of the second month. The four-, five- and seven-year T-notes are auctioned on different days once a quarter.

However, the purchase procedure is identical to T-bills. New issues can be bought directly from the U.S. Government through the Treasury Direct plan described in Key 5, or from Federal Reserve banks and their branches or from brokerage houses. T-notes that have already been issued can be bought and resold in the secondary market.

Who are the prime customers for treasury notes? I've found that banks are the big buyers, although individuals and managers of small portfolios favor them because they can deliver a little higher yield in exchange for going out a little further on the maturity scale. Although the exact differential depends on the shape of the yield curve, four-year T-notes historically have delivered 1¼ percent higher yield than three-month T-bills, according to Benham Capital Management, a Palo Alto, California, mutual fund management company with several funds specializing in Treasury securities.

Nevertheless, T-notes have the same great flexibility and liquidity of T-bills and T-bonds because they, too, can be sold before maturity into that very active secondary market. The flip side of the coin is that investors can go into that secondary market and buy a T-note, again through a brokerage firm, with a three-month maturity, avoid price fluctuations, have access to ready cash, and perhaps earn a greater rate of return than by owning a T-bill.

However, that strategy really works only for investors with a tremendous amount of cash—$1 million or more. The reason: institutions generally buy those close-to-maturity higher yielding notes. On top of that, the brokerage fees on those T-notes would offset the higher yields—which means that smaller investors who want to stay short should stick with T-bills.

T-notes also have their own personality. They are not callable. That means the Treasury cannot retire the debt before maturity at terms that are favorable to the U.S.

Government and therefore shortchange investors. This is a king-sized advantage treasuries have over corporate bonds, and its importance shouldn't be downplayed. Companies issuing bonds with call features will retrieve them out of investor hands without warning if interest payments on the high yield are squeezing their cash flow or if the company feels it can issue new bonds with lower interest rates.

7

T-NOTES FOR INCOME INVESTING

Treasury notes can be an excellent financial planning tool for hold-to-maturity investors looking for a steady stream of interest for up to ten years at a yield generally above T-bill rates.

But it is impossible to talk in absolutes. There are some facts of life—and investing strategies—that most investors are not aware of when it comes to treasury notes. Understanding them will give you the edge over other investors.

First, once a treasury note is issued, there is no way to tell whether it is a T-note or a T-bond except by its maturity. (T-notes, as mentioned earlier, have a maximum maturity of ten years.) People are either "bill" investors or "bond" investors; there are very few, if any, who consider themselves "note" investors. The term "T-note" merely reflects the fact that these are mid-range government securities. Even the newspaper quotations each day do not differentiate between a T-note and a T-bond in their tables.

Second, depending on your financial objectives, you can buy a T-note selling for a premium—above par—and often get higher current yield. Why? Because so-called "premium notes" carry coupons with greater-than-market-rate interest, hence they often sell for more than 100 cents on the dollar. More income, but little or no capital appreciation.

Buying a high coupon or premium T-note is actually a wise strategy if you are bearish on the bond market. If interest rates do go up, you realize more income to reinvest at the higher rates. Plus, the high yield of a premium T-note cushions a price fall when interest rates climb. Why? Because the higher yield throws off more reinvestment dollars, and those notes are in demand.

A solid strategy for bond market bulls is to buy a low coupon or discount treasury note. Because these T-notes have coupons paying at less than the market rate, they sell at a discount, sometimes a deep one. In addition, the older the issue, the wider the bid and ask spread, making these notes less liquid, less easily traded. Hence, the demand for them is lower. But when interest rates drop, discounted T-notes surge in price. If you hold to maturity, you may realize less coupon income, but there's greater capital appreciation.

Meanwhile, there are some "benchmarks" used by sophisticated T-note investors. Jeff Tyler, portfolio manager of the Benham Treasury Note Fund, says he looks for a "historical premium" between a T-note yield and the rate of inflation. Typically, T-note yields should be three percentage points over the inflation rate.

Tyler looks at it this way. If you expect a constant inflationary rate of 5 percent to remain in effect, then an 8.5 percent yield on a T-note would represent an added value of 50 basis points (or one half of one percent). However, if you believe inflation will rise to 6 or 6.5 percent, then an 8.5 percent yield would not be as attractive an investment.

Tyler also advises investors to make their T-note purchases just before or after an auction. Here's why. Right before a Treasury auction, institutions will want to get into the newest treasury security, so they will often sell the treasuries they bought at the prior auction to generate liquidity. This is especially true for the two-year T-note, which is auctioned monthly. By unloading, the market will be flooded with a stream of these maturities, and the oversupply of these older issues often depresses their prices and creates buying opportunities for astute investors.

At the same time, newly auctioned treasuries in the most popular maturities—two to seven years—command a premium because of their liquidity. So, if the oversupply of the existing two-year T-notes has reduced their price, and the highly liquid newly auctioned T-notes sell at a premium, it's your chance to capitalize on one of the most venerable economic theories—an imbalance of supply and demand pushes down price. That's your chance to pounce.

8

THE SAFETY OF A TREASURY INSTRUMENT

For generations, the treasury bond was a granite-like symbol of security that arrived as an ornately engraved certificate suitable for framing but was normally kept in a safe-deposit box. This was the ultimate U.S. Government IOU, a loan to the Treasury Department for 30 years, guaranteed to be repaid with interest in the form of semiannual coupon payments. The T-bond was as good as gold. Better, in fact, because it paid a yield.

It is still a rock-solid investment, yet it has changed somewhat with the times. Treasury bonds, with the longest maturity and usually the highest yield compared with other treasury securities, are no longer issued in bearer form. The engraved certificate, known as a "bearer bond," was expensive to produce and difficult to replace if lost. Bearer bonds, the equivalent of cash, are too cumbersome to handle. Plus, holders of bearer bonds must detach or "clip" the coupons and redeem them for cash at a commercial bank, a Federal Reserve bank, or one of its branches—a hassle in today's world, where time is a precious commodity. In 1986, bearer bonds were phased out, although there are plenty that have not yet matured and are still in circulation.

Instead, T-bonds and T-notes are now issued in "registered form." The owner's name is typed on the face of the certificate and registered on the books or, more accurately, in the Treasury Department computers. If the T-bond is lost, stolen, or destroyed, there is a permanent ownership record. And instead of clipping coupons and trudging to a bank to cash them in, you receive semi-annual interest payments directly from the Treasury.

Fundamentally, though, the T-bond remains the same. It is issued in denominations as low as $1,000 and in increments of $5,000, $10,000, $100,000, $1 million, $100 million, and $500 million. There is a single maturity—30 years—hence it's known as the "long bond." Like T-bills and T-notes, the coupon interest on T-bonds is exempt from state and local income taxes but is subject to federal income tax. (Of course, realized gains from any price appreciation must be reported as income on federal and state returns.)

T-bonds, like T-bills and T-notes, can also be purchased at auction through the Treasury Direct program at no cost. You make a noncompetitive bid, which means you accept the price and interest rate established by the auction. To buy direct, you submit a "tender" (actually a gold-colored form number PD 5174-4) and payment to one of the 12 Federal Reserve banks or one of its branches, or directly to the Bureau of Public Debt in Washington. Mailed bids must be postmarked no later than the day before the auction date and received prior to the issue date. To avoid snags, it's wise to mark the envelope "Tender for Treasury Bonds" in the bottom-left corner of the envelope.

Newly auctioned T-bonds are also sold by commercial banks, usually for a flat fee of $25 to $50, or from investment brokerage firms.

In reality, comparatively few individual investors buy treasury bonds at auctions these days and sock them away for three decades without touching them. In today's world, most yield-sensitive buy-and-hold investors are going toward shorter maturities to maximize their coupon income. Savers who want to lock up high rates generally lean toward bank certificates of deposit because they're considered convenient. Yet, the long-term CD is absolute folly because you lose liquidity and flexibility the minute you put your money away.

Instead, if you are a saver wanting a high yield to maturity and the assurance of total safety, you should not overlook the 30-year T-bond, and there is one very good reason for this: You can sell out in an instant if you need the money, and you pay no "early withdrawal" penalties, those expensive fees usually levied by banks and savings and loans for breaking into a certificate of deposit before maturity. If you sell your T-bond in the secondary market, you'll pay a fraction of a commission and be in a cash position within minutes. Indeed, the liquidity of the secondary market for T-bonds is as appealing to savers and investors as the Treasury Department's guarantees of zero credit risk.

Nevertheless, that strategy is not without financial risk. To liquidate T-bonds before maturity, you must sell them into the secondary market at the current bid price—a price that may be less than the price you paid. The 30-year T-bond, being at the extreme end of the yield curve, is subject to greater market risk than any other treasury security. When interest rates move, the price of a 30-year T-bond will fluctuate more than the price of a one-year T-bill. Why? Because the extended maturity makes a basis point worth more the farther out you go on the yield curve. (See Key 12 on the yield curve.)

9

THE MOST VOLATILE TREASURIES

The 30-year treasury bond can experience price swings so severe that few individual investors trade it. I personally stay with intermediate treasuries like the five-year or seven-year T-note to minimize price volatility. Or, I will trade T-bond futures on the Chicago Board of Trade. (See Key 17.)

Who, then, buys the long bond and for what reason? Perhaps 95 percent of the players in the T-bond market are institutions that possess the steel nerves needed to withstand the price fluctuations and have a long-term financial obligation to meet. The big buyers of 30-year bonds are life insurance companies and pension funds; both have to deliver cash at some future date and T-bonds, bought and held to maturity, are an asset that offsets that liability.

In addition to the guaranteed return, institutions that need a long-term debt instrument do not have to worry about having a treasury called away before maturity. Unlike corporate bonds, including even AAA-rated corporates, most T-bonds have a noncallable provision.

Other T-bond buyers are primary dealers who may strip off their coupons and resell them as zero-coupon bonds to investors who want to use them to fund Individual Retirement Accounts (IRAs), Keogh Plans for self-employed individuals, and other tax-advantaged (qualified) retirement plans. Additional buyers include portfolio managers of mutual funds holding U.S. Government securities. Banks generally buy treasuries when their loan volume sags, but they usually stick with shorter maturities. Banks would rather forgo a few basis points in yield to avoid the price volatility of the longer bond.

Even investors who do not buy the long bond watch it like a hawk. Its yield to maturity is considered to be the prevailing long-term interest rate. That's why it is often called the "benchmark bond;" it reflects the true cost of money.

There are some important characteristics and behavioral traits of the newly issued 30-year T-bond that every investor should know. For openers, the newest issues are usually the most actively traded and are called "on-the-run" bonds. Spreads between their bid and ask prices are often two to four basis points lower than a comparable, older T-bond because investors are paying for the liquidity. As the T-bond ages, it's referred to by the number of years remaining before it matures: An original 30-year bond with five years to go before the Treasury must redeem it becomes a "five-year bond."

The 30-year T-bond is, however, a favorite of the very aggressive trader looking for leverage. You can buy long bonds on margin for about 10 percent down with the brokerage firm financing the balance but retaining physical possession of the bonds as collateral. Leveraging the volatile 30-year T-bond is a risky strategy. If interest rates move up sharply, the price of bonds will drop just as quickly. If the value falls significantly, you may be forced to ante up more cash within a few hours. Or the brokerage firm may sell you out of your position and you could lose part or all of your original cash down payment.

Professional investors use the long bond for various trading strategies, including yield curve arbitrage. For example, if you think short-term interest rates will drop faster than long-term rates, you would short the 30-year bond and buy a two-year treasury note.

Portfolio managers use T-bonds primarily for liquidity. Fern Barrasso, an assistant vice president who trades treasuries for Aetna Bond Investors, a subsidiary of Aetna Life and Casualty Insurance Company, has anywhere from 5 percent to 25 percent of Aetna's fixed income portfolio invested in treasuries of differing maturities at any one time. "We use the long treasuries as a surrogate guarantee for very long liabilities until we can find a higher yielding fixed income security, either a corporate bond or a private placement investment with a higher yield," she says. And because she uses treasuries essentially as a parking place for cash with no intention of holding to maturity, Barrasso says she buys the least expensive surrogate (treasury) she can find.

Even though buy/ask spreads are thin on big blocks of treasuries, Barrasso shops the market hard. She calls four primary dealers to let their brokers know she's "shopping." Within 30 seconds, all are back with their offer price. Since she is, again, only using the T-bond to "plug a temporary hole" in her bond portfolio, she opts for the lowest price.

Barrasso says the typical commission for on-the-run long bonds is a "half" ($1/32$ of a point) or a "plus" ($1/64$ of a point) so she realizes that primary dealers "are not making a ton of money on these transactions." What they are often after, she contends, is "current information" they can use to manage their own fixed income inventories and investment portfolios or market and pricing intelligence that they must feed to the Fed every week.

Most professional traders do not advise individuals to buy the 30-year T-bond for anything less than a hold to maturity strategy simply because it requires constant monitoring. Even mutual fund portfolio managers will use the long bond when they are convinced interest rates are going to drop. "Then we'll buy off-the-run issues because they tend to yield more, and we'll sit on them for six months," explains Jim Kellerman, managing director of Criterion Group, a Houston-based mutual fund group with $10 billion under management. (Criterion Group is a subsidiary of the Transamerica Corporation.)

As for individual investors who choose to invest in treasuries direct and not through a mutual fund, Kellerman suggests no more than two-year maturities purchased direct from a Federal Reserve bank. Buying T-bonds in small amounts in the secondary market is prohibitively expensive from a commission standpoint. Individuals may pay half a percent while institutions with their purchasing power and clout as repeat customers get those wafer-thin commissions of $1/64$ to $1/256$ of a percentage point.

The bottom line on the T-bond? There are dozens of trading strategies on how and when to use them. But unless you have at least $100,000 to commit to the long bond and the time, expertise, and steel-plated stomach to pick off profits while riding out roller-coastering price fluctuations, stick with shorter maturities. The extra yield usually generated by the volatile long bond isn't worth the anxieties suffered when it's your own money at risk.

10

ZERO-COUPON GOVERNMENTS: THE PROS AND CONS OF "STRIPS"

Zero-coupon bonds, at first blush, sound like a worthless investment. If there is no coupon, hence no yield, why would anyone invest solely for the potential of price appreciation?

The fact is, zeros pay no income during the life of the bond, but there is an interest rate quoted and a payoff—when the bond matures. In fact, because there is no coupon attached to the bond, and no periodic interest payments, zeros sell at a deep discount from par. So, when you couple the price appreciation with the interest paid at maturity, the gains can be whopping.

First, a little background. Zero-coupon bonds can either be corporates or treasuries. In both cases, the dealer has taken a conventional bond and stripped it of its interest coupons. The difference is that zero treasuries, unlike corporates, have no credit risk. Just like a normal T-bond, they are backed by the full faith and credit of the U.S. Government. They come in denominations as low as $1,000 (but since they're discounted, they sell for far less) and, like regular T-bonds, are issued in maturities that go out as far as 30 years.

In recent years, zero or "stripped" treasuries have acquired some exotic names. Wall Streeters normally call them STRIPS, an acronym for Separate Trading of Registered Interest and Principal of Securities. (STRIPS were actually created by the Treasury Department and the Federal Reserve Bank.) Earlier, Merrill Lynch trotted out TIGRs, short for Treasury Investors Growth Receipts.

Lehman Brothers, now known as Shearson Lehman Hutton, followed with LIONs (Lehman Investment Opportunity Notes), while Salomon Brothers started selling CATS (Certificate of Accrual on Treasury Securities).

Regardless of what they are called, zero treasuries have one drawback: Investors pay income tax each year on the growing principal and interest. In other words, while you are not collecting any coupon income, you're taxed on that year's prorated portion.

As a result, investors should only consider zero treasuries as an investment for a tax-free or qualified plan. That's one reason that pension funds and other institutional-sized tax-exempt investors have been big fans of zero treasuries. Individuals can accumulate them in Individual Retirement Accounts (IRAs) and Keogh Plans and avoid paying income tax on the coupon income realized that year and on any price appreciation. However, they will pay federal and any applicable state taxes when they retire and withdraw the funds.

Apart from being taxed along the way until maturity, zeros—both treasuries and corporates—have another failing. Unless you hold them until maturity, you never collect a dime of the coupon interest. Indeed, zero treasuries are almost identical to T-bills in one big respect: They sell at a discount and interest isn't paid until they mature and are cashed in. Sure, like T-bills, you can sell zero treasuries before the maturity date and there is an active secondary trading market with plenty of liquidity.

So, you see, zero or stripped treasuries are like a double-edged sword. One edge has this enticing, enormous guaranteed profit owing to the deep discount from the face value. For a one-time cash payment of $172, a stripped treasury with a 9 percent interest rate is guaranteed to mature at $1,000 in 20 years.

The other edge of the sword requires you to pay taxes on "phantom" income every year. Yet, if interest rates climb, you have no coupon income to invest at the higher levels as you would with a conventional bond. In short, to collect your coupon income, you have to hold to maturity for your lump sum payoff.

11

STRIPPED TREASURIES: SHOPPING HARD BEFORE YOU BUY

In the past, zero or stripped treasuries had some alluring benefits that often persuaded investors to hold to maturity. At one point, zero treasury yields were slightly higher than couponed bonds and during the years of double-digit interest rates, investors could lock in some towering rates, often tax-free. Second, old tax laws allowed investors to use zeros to fund a college education for their children.

In those days youngsters, regardless of age, were taxed according to the level of their own income. Obviously, this placed most children in a rock-bottom bracket and parents had to make only minimal cash outlays at tax time. But when the Tax Reform Act of 1986 was passed, the new law said that youngsters under 14 were to be taxed at their parent's bracket; at 14 or over, they were to be taxed according to their own income. That threw a monkey wrench into a great strategy: buying zeros with staggered maturities for a newborn. That way the first bond would mature in 18 years to coincide with the child's freshman year in college, and the remainder matured in the three successive years, just in time to make tuition payments.

The concept is still valid. It's known on Wall Street as "matching liabilities"—creating a lump sum of cash to meet a massive payment, and a few people are still using zeros as a forced-saving strategy to underwrite the cost of college while paying the taxes along the way. That may work for a teenager 14 and up if parents feel a zero treasury makes economic sense after taxes. However, anyone with extremely young children might want to explore Series EE Bonds (see Keys 24 and 25) where there are new tax benefits for what are called "education bonds."

Nevertheless, zero treasuries still have enormous appeal to a variety of investors. The problem is that brokers know this, and some will load up the quote with various fees, markups, and commissions. A favorite ploy among some brokers is to tell a zero-bond customer that there is no commission when there really is, but it's just hidden. A commission, technically, is an up-front sales charge. However, the brokerage firm's institutional trading desk usually just adds a markup to the net price of the bond, and the customer is none the wiser.

To be on the safe side, shop around. Get at least five different quotes from five brokers, and you will be amazed at the variance among zero prices because some brokerages have zeros in inventory while others have to buy from a government bond dealer. As for commissions, while they should never be more than 1 percent of the face amount of the zero treasuries, hopefully they will actually be only one quarter of 1 percent. Ask the broker to break out the cost and the commissions or extra costs. And if you're told the purchase is commission-free, you can bet the broker is getting compensated with a credit, often one eighth of 1 percent, back from the trading desk.

This is also an opportunity to find out if your broker is actually working on your behalf. Zero treasuries are not a commonly requested investment, and if you are told your broker can't really get you the best offering and you are pointed to another source—don't be surprised. The pros operate that way and you'll know you have a person looking out for your net worth.

There are some specific investment strategies that work well with zero or stripped treasuries. For instance, if you think interest rates will rise over the next ten years, buy one bond due in five years. When that matures, buy another five-year zero, which hopefully will be at a higher rate.

But if you expect interest rates to be volatile but basically bullish in future years, a so-called "long strip"—a 30-year zero T-bond—will often outperform a 30-year couponed T-bond in its rate of return on your money; long strips sell at a very steep discount from face value. On the other hand, a strategy for bears is to buy a one- or two-year "short strip" and remain liquid for reinvestment purposes.

12

HOW THE YIELD CURVE CAN SET YOU STRAIGHT

The yield curve is a great decision-making tool for people investing in U.S. Treasury securities. But it is also a difficult concept for investors to grasp because there are no ironclad rules for interpreting the curve. The yield curve is probably best described as a fairly reliable barometer for predicting the price risks—and rewards—in holding government securities to their maturity date.

What exactly is the yield curve? It is a chart or diagram showing the yields and maturities of identical fixed income securities plotted over time.

You will not find a yield curve in the *Wall Street Journal* or in your daily newspaper. But it can be drawn, or plotted, based on the quotations found in the chart headed "Treasury Bonds, Notes and Bills" in those same newspapers. Now, before we chart our yield curve and make our investment decisions, let's recall some truisms for fixed income investments.

It's generally believed that prices fluctuate more on debt securities with longer maturities. No one can forecast the future, but investors willing to buy a 30-year bond should theoretically be compensated for tying up their money for a long time, enduring price volatility, and gambling on the creditworthiness of the instrument itself. Will that debt instrument pay off the holder at maturity?

With a U.S. Treasury security—a T-bill, note, or bond—one worry is eliminated. Treasuries theoretically have no credit risk because they're backed by the full faith and credit of the U.S. Government. But holders still face the same risk of fluctuating prices as interest rates themselves change. Our principal risk is price fluctuation and that largely depends on interest rates—whether the Federal Reserve is pumping money into the economy or tightening the flow—and investor expectations.

To construct your own yield curve, plot the current on-the-run issues on the horizontal axis of a graph and the yields on the vertical axis. The exact securities that qualify as "on-the-runs" change as new bonds, notes, and bills are issued, although the standard maturities are generally three months, six months, one year, two years, three years, four years, five years, seven years, ten years, and 30 years.

The yield curve graph on the next page is based on the *Wall Street Journal* of October 1, 1990, and shows a positive slope.

In plotting these yields on a piece of paper, you will see a yield curve that slopes upward, or positively. Why? Because short-term interest rates are generally lower than long-term interest rates. The rising yield forecasts the additional income you will make taking the extra risk of owning T-notes with a longer maturity. The challenge for investors is to find that one point on the curve where they feel comfortable with the yield from the treasury note (or bill) without sensing they are locked in and unable to take advantage of more attractive yields offered by other treasury issues—whether bills, bonds, or notes.

But the wild card in plotting the yield curve and making investment decisions is investor expectations. A positively sloped yield curve says the prevailing opinion is that interest rates will climb in the future, but investors mistakenly buy long-term treasuries for the fattest yield. Instead, they should be buying the short-term bonds and rolling them over at maturity—renewing them at a higher yield.

The secret is to look out on the horizon of a positive yield curve, regardless of how steep it becomes, to find that point where you get maximum return with minimum worry.

Sample Yield Curve
(as of September 28, 1990)

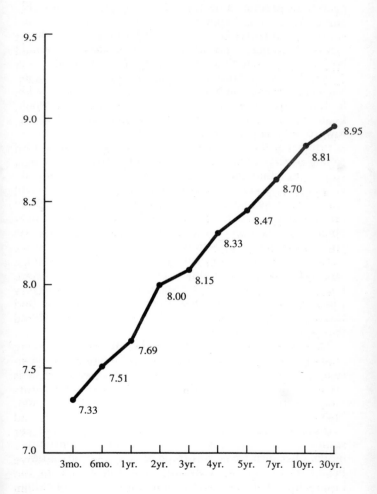

But not all yield curves slope positively. When short-term interest rates are higher than long-term rates, that usually indicates the market is expecting interest rates to decline sometime in the near future. These fears or expectations produce a negatively sloping or inverted yield curve. When this happens, investors generally buy the shortest maturities, again hoping to grab the highest yields. Once again, they are making a mistake and should be buying intermediate or longer-term maturities.

Why? Because both of the gut reactions—investing in long maturities in the face of a positive yield curve and looking short when the curve turns negative—are what I call "herd instinct" mistakes. Everyone starts galloping toward what appears to be the same refuge and the market outfoxes them at maturity. When it comes time for rolling over your money into the more attractive yields, you cannot find them available. In a positively sloped yield curve, you're locked into a lower yield and your money isn't available to take advantage of the higher rates. Indeed, experience has taught me that when the obvious appears to be the smartest choice, it's wise to go in the opposite direction.

The yield curve can also be flat. That means short-term interest rates are almost equal to long-term rates. For the past few years, we've seen a flat yield curve, which means the market has no expectations for the future course of interest rates and is essentially predicting that a drifting market lies ahead.

To summarize, expectations—what the market thinks is going to happen to interest rates—produce a horizontal (flat) yield curve when interest rates are stable, an upward-sloping yield curve when interest rates are low, and a downward-sloping yield curve when interest rates are high.

It's a mistake, though, to picture the yield curve as static—negative, positive, or flat. The curve is constantly moving because treasuries trade almost 24 hours a day. For example, an inverted yield curve that is starting to lose its inversion is usually a bullish sign heralding rising bond prices. Why? Short-term rates are starting to fall relative to long rates, thus indicating an easing of monetary policy by the Federal Reserve Board. And when rates drop, both prices, moving inversely, climb. Essentially, the market is changing its attitudes, perceptions, feelings, and inflationary expectations and is looking for deflation.

The flip side of the coin is just as dramatic. When the positively sloped yield curve starts to lose its steepness, short-term rates rise. The market is anticipating the Fed tightening the faucet on the money flow, borrowing subsides, and inflation fears take hold.

The bottom line? The yield curve is not a fail-safe forecaster of how treasury prices will perform. But it is probably the best yardstick you have for maximizing your yield while maintaining your liquidity before a bond matures.

13

HOW TO FIND A BOND BROKER

Not all investment brokers are alike. Stockbrokers, often called "account executives," are supervised by a sales manager and usually must generate a certain commission income quota. Hence, the stocks they recommend are often part of a brokerage firm's inventory—shares their firm may have underwritten or their research department is recommending. Account executives must move that stock.

A good stockbroker is rarely a specialist in treasuries or the fixed income market. It is virtually impossible to be an expert in both stocks and bonds. Bond brokers usually have a broader grasp on global markets and world economies, and they must be skilled in forecasting the direction and behavior of short- and long-term interest rates. Interest rates, as I've said earlier, drive the price and yields of treasuries and all fixed income securities.

Bond brokers have no "market tape" to follow to track up-to-the-second trades and instead work from a series of "screens." For that reason, you must make sure that any broker you choose to work with has access to these Telerate or Bloomberg screens. Otherwise, your broker will lag the market and your executions will suffer.

There are also differences among bond brokers. Those who work for large investment houses, like stockbrokers, are usually advised by their management to sell from their "inventory." They rarely "shop the street" to track down the precise treasury instrument at the exact rate, maturity, and price to fit the client's need. It is the investment business equivalent to buying off the rack.

However, an independent bond broker with no ties to any major brokerage organization is free to shop other firms—that is, other broker/dealers—to see what they have in their inventories and what the price may be. Because prices, commissions, and markups vary, it is important to find an energetic broker who will work on your behalf—even if it takes "shopping" five or six other firms to track down the best transaction for you.

Finding a good bond broker is not that easy. First, find a broker who is a successful investor for his or her own account. That's right. You want to work with someone who does not see you as a source of income, a new commission-generating account. Of course, brokers are not so benevolent that they work without compensation, but you don't want them to be living off your portfolio either. Ask the general manager of a brokerage firm near you: "Who is the most successful bond broker in your office?"

Avoid the "broker of the day" system wherein new account executives are assigned the "walk-ins" (or the call-ins).

Next, arrange a meeting. There are several things to look for, and you'll spot them or feel them ten minutes after you arrive at the broker's office. Find out if he or she is organized and backed up with a support staff to handle clerical requests from you or your accountant. Your bond broker should also take the time and interest to pass along information such as articles, rulings, and research that can help you in your investment decision-making.

Is the personal chemistry right? Does this broker make you feel comfortable? Are your questions encouraged or simply tolerated? Is there any arrogance in the broker's voice?

Now comes question-and-answer time. And *both* of you should ask some probing questions. Find out whether prospective brokers have put their own money on the line and have followed their own recommendations. Ask for client references as well and check them out. Look for long-term relationships. Has the broker been in the business at least ten years, through good markets and bad?

Expect brokers to ask *you* some rather penetrating questions, too. Are you conservative or aggressive? Trying to build capital or generate income? What are your current investment and personal financial goals? The best brokers will try to see exactly where you stand on the risk/reward spectrum so they can tailor investment advice exactly to your personal objectives. Do they answer your questions thoroughly? How do they react when you ask about commissions, markups, fees? The better brokers will take the time to walk you through a transaction, explaining it every step of the way. Will they refer you to top-performing no-load mutual funds even though they reap no commission?

Remember, you are not marrying your broker. If the relationship is not working, end it, and move on to another one. After all, it's your money.

14

HOW TO READ THE FINANCIAL PAGES

The financial pages of any major newspaper serve up a buffet of information to the investor who wants to track treasuries as well as other economic market trends.

Locate the quotation tables of treasury bonds, notes, and bills and begin by examining the first three columns for a full description of the security you are considering. As an example, the first column of the table on the next page shows an 8⅛ percent note of Aug 92 which means a $1,000 note will pay $81.25 annually, or 8⅛ percent × $1,000.

The second and third columns give the maturity date of the bond or note by month and year; when two or more years are listed here, it means the security matures on the later date but could be called (or redeemed) by the Treasury as early as the first date, in order to reissue the debt at a lower coupon if market rates drop. If there is an "n" listed after the month, the security was issued as a note; a "p" indicates that the note is exempt from withholding tax if bought by a nonresident. The fourth and fifth columns quote the prices that buyers were bidding and sellers were asking on the date for which the statistics are listed. These prices are quoted in 32nds for bonds and notes and in 100ths for bills and reflect a percentage of par (or $1,000 value) for the security. In other words, for that same 8⅛ percent note due in August 1992, at the close of trading on Friday, September 28, buyers were bidding 100⁵/₃₂ of par value ($1,000 × 1.0016 = $1,001.60) while sellers of that security were asking for 100⁷/₃₂ ($1,000 × 1.0022 = $1,002.20).

The sixth column reflects the change in bid price, again

41

Treasury Bonds, Notes & Bills

GOVT. BONDS & NOTES

Rate	Maturity	Bid	Asked	Bid Chg.	Yld.
11 1/2	Oct 90n	100:04	100:06	....	5.90
8 1/4	Oct 90n	100:01	100:03	+ 1	6.82
8	Nov 90n	100:00	100:02	....	7.25
7 7/8	Aug 92n	99:21	99:25	+ 3	8.00
8 1/4	Aug 92n	100:11	100:15	+ 4	7.98
8 1/8	Aug 92n	100:05	100:07	+ 2	8.00
8 1/8	Sep 92n*	100:06	100:08	+ 2	7.99
8 3/4	Sep 92n	101:09	101:13	+ 2	7.97
9 3/4	Oct 92n	103:04	103:08	+ 3	7.99
7 3/4	Nov 92n	99:11	99:15	+ 4	8.03
8 3/8	Nov 92n	100:17	100:21	+ 3	8.03
10 1/2	Nov 92n	104:19	104:23	+ 4	8.04
9 1/8	Dec 92n	102:02	102:06	+ 3	8.04
8 3/4	Jan 93n	101:12	101:16	+ 6	8.02
4	Feb 88-93	94:11	95:11	− 5	6.14
6 3/4	Feb 93	97:05	97:13	+ 7	7.97
7 7/8	Feb 93	99:20	99:28	+ 7	7.93
8 1/4	Feb 93n	100:08	100:10	+ 5	8.10
8 3/8	Feb 93n	100:17	100:19	+ 6	8.09
10 7/8	Feb 93n	105:25	105:29	+ 6	8.09
9 5/8	Mar 93n	103:10	103:14	+ 6	8.08
7 3/8	Apr 93n	98:08	98:12	+ 6	8.10
7 5/8	May 93n	98:23	98:27	+ 6	8.12
8 5/8	May 93n	101:02	101:04	+ 6	8.14
10 1/8	May 93n	104:16	104:20	+ 6	8.13
8 1/8	Jun 93n	99:29	100:01	+ 6	8.11
7 1/4	Jul 93n	97:23	97:27	+ 7	8.13
7 1/2	Aug 88-93	98:08	98:16	+ 7	8.10
8	Aug 93n	99:18	99:20	+ 7	8.15
8 5/8	Aug 93	101:03	101:11	+ 7	8.09
8 3/4	Aug 93n	101:12	101:16	+ 6	8.15
11 7/8	Aug 93n	109:06	109:10	+ 6	8.17
9 1/2	May 94n	103:16	103:20	+ 7	8.32
13 1/8	May 94n	114:17	114:21	+ 8	8.35
8 1/2	Jun 94n	100:15	100:17	+ 7	8.33
8	Jul 94n	98:27	98:31	+ 7	8.32
8 5/8	Aug 94n	100:24	100:28	+ 7	8.36
8 3/4	Aug 94	101:06	101:10	+ 8	8.35
10 1/2	Aug 95n	107:23	107:27	+ 10	8.50
8 5/8	Oct 95n	100:12	100:16	+ 8	8.50
8 1/2	Nov 95n	100:01	100:03	+ 7	8.47
9 1/2	Nov 95n	103:28	104:00	+ 10	8.52
11 1/2	Nov 95	111:29	112:01	+ 10	8.55
9 1/4	Jan 96n	102:27	102:31	+ 10	8.54
8 7/8	Feb 96n	101:09	101:13	+ 10	8.54
8 1/2	Apr 97n	99:01	99:05	+ 14	8.67
8 1/2	May 97n	98:31	99:03	+ 13	8.68
8 1/2	Jul 97n	98:30	99:00	+ 13	8.70
8 5/8	Aug 97n	99:16	99:20	+ 13	8.70
8 7/8	Nov 97n	100:23	100:27	+ 14	8.71
8 1/8	Feb 98n	96:21	96:25	+ 14	8.73
7	May 93-98	90:02	90:10	+ 13	8.77
9	May 98n	101:09	101:13	+ 12	8.74
9 1/4	Aug 98n	102:18	102:22	+ 15	8.77
3 1/2	Nov 98	93:07	94:07	+ 5	4.35
8 7/8	Nov 98n	100:15	100:19	+ 17	8.77
8 7/8	Feb 99n	100:13	100:17	+ 16	8.78
8 1/2	May 94-99	98:02	98:10	+ 13	8.78
9 1/8	May 99n	101:26	101:30	+ 18	8.80
8	Aug 99n	95:01	95:05	+ 16	8.80
7 7/8	Nov 99n	94:05	94:07	+ 17	8.81
7 7/8	Feb 95-00	93:27	93:31	+ 16	8.83
8 1/2	Feb 00n	97:30	98:02	+ 16	8.81
8 7/8	May 00n	100:05	100:07	+ 15	8.84
8 3/8	Aug 95-00	96:26	96:30	+ 15	8.85
8 3/4	Aug 00n	99:17	99:19	+ 17	8.81
11 3/4	Feb 01	119:08	119:16	+ 22	8.84
13 1/8	May 01	128:30	129:06	+ 23	8.83
8	Aug 96-01	94:00	94:08	+ 12	8.83
8 1/2	Feb 20	95:08	95:12	+ 27	8.95
8 3/4	May 20	97:27	97:31	+ 30	8.95
8 3/4	Aug 20	97:28	97:30	+ 29	8.95

U.S. TREASURY STRIPS

Mat.	Type	Bid	Asked	Chg.	Bid Yld.
Nov 90	ci	99:03	99:03	− 1	7.57
Feb 91	ci	97:07	97:07	....	7.73
May 91	ci	95:13	95:13	....	7.75

TREASURY BILLS

Maturity	Days to Mat.	Bid	Asked	Chg.	Ask Yld.
Oct 04 '90	6	6.09	6.01	+0.17	6.10
Oct 11 '90	13	6.50	6.48	+0.36	6.58
Dec 13 '90	76	7.15	7.13	−0.09	7.33
Dec 20 '90	83	7.14	7.12	−0.11	7.33
Dec 27 '90	90	7.14	7.12	−0.09	7.34
Jan 03 '91	97	7.13	7.11	−0.08	7.34
Mar 14 '91	167	7.19	7.17	−0.05	7.51
Mar 21 '91	174	7.18	7.16	−0.08	7.51
Mar 28 '91	181	7.17	7.15	−0.06	7.51
Apr 11 '91	195	7.16	7.14	−0.04	7.51
May 09 '91	223	7.26	7.24	−0.05	7.63
Jun 06 '91	251	7.21	7.19	−0.05	7.59
Jul 05 '91	280	7.27	7.25	−0.05	7.68
Aug 01 '91	307	7.26	7.24	−0.03	7.70
Aug 29 '91	335	7.22	7.20	−0.04	7.69
Sep 26 '91	363	7.17	7.15	−0.03	7.66

expressed in 32nds for bonds and notes and in 100ths for bills, from the prior day's close.

The final column lists the yield to maturity.

Understanding the role that treasury securities play in your portfolio often hinges on a few mathematical formulae. Some are too complex to walk through here, but others are simple to grasp and implement. (For reference purposes, the long bond, 8¾ percent of August 2020, as listed in the October 1, 1990 *Wall Street Journal,* is used for these examples.)

The following calculation will give you the approximate yield on T-notes or T-bonds selling below or above par. If they sell at par, the coupon rate and the current yield will be the same.

$$\text{Current Yield} = \frac{\text{Coupon payments}}{\text{Market price}}$$
$$= \frac{\$87.50}{\$978.75}$$
$$= .0894$$
$$= 8.94\%$$

$$\begin{array}{l}\text{Approximate} \\ \text{Yield to} \\ \text{Maturity}\end{array} = \frac{\text{Annual coupon payment} + \left(\begin{array}{c}\text{Face} \\ \text{value}\end{array} - \begin{array}{c}\text{Market} \\ \text{price}\end{array}\right)/\begin{array}{c}\text{No. of years} \\ \text{to maturity}\end{array}}{(\text{Face value} + \text{Market value})/2}$$
$$= \frac{\$87.50 + (1{,}000 - 978.80)/30}{(\$1{,}000 + 978.80)/2}$$
$$= \frac{\$87.50 + \$21.20/30}{\$1978.80/2}$$
$$= \frac{\$88.21}{\$989.40}$$
$$= .0892$$
$$= 8.92\%$$

For treasury bills, the following calculations will help you understand how these discount securities may fit your investment needs. (For reference purposes, the bill due December 20, 1990, as listed on the preceding page is used for the following calculations.)

$$\text{Discount} = \frac{\dfrac{\text{Ask price}}{100} \times 10,000}{360} \times \text{Days to maturity}$$

Discount Rate (Yield)

$$= \frac{\text{Discount}}{\text{Par value}} \times \text{Time multiplier}$$

$$= \frac{\$164.16}{\$10,000} \times \frac{360}{83}$$

$$= .016416 \times 4.34$$

$$= .0712$$

$$= 7.12\%$$

Yield to Maturity

$$= \frac{\text{Discount}}{\text{Purchase price}} \times \text{Time factor}$$

$$= \frac{164.16}{9835.84} \times \frac{365}{83}$$

$$= .01667 \times 4.40$$

$$= .0734$$

$$= 7.34\%$$

15

BUILDING A CONSENSUS VIEW OF THE MARKET

Perhaps the wisest strategy if you do not plan to hold treasuries to maturity but are looking for capital appreciation is to form your own consensus view of the market. Your goal is to anticipate just what the market is expecting from certain key economic indicators before the numbers are announced. This takes doing enough homework on the economy to develop your own personal hunches. Or you can even buy a consensus from various professional marketwatchers. A Belmont, California, company called MMS International is a prime example of a consensus finder. One of its services, a great tool for serious investors in treasuries, is its weekly survey of primary dealers and economists in the United States, Asia, and Europe.

"The serious investor has to gear up for what the bond market is expecting from major economic releases that week," maintains Kermit Claytor, who edits several of the firm's monetary newsletters. He says the MMS survey is designed to provide investors with a "median expectation" of what the market anticipates hearing so they can formulate buy, sell, or hedge decisions that will move with the market.

This point cannot be emphasized strongly enough. Call it a consensus, call it an expectation, but the bottom line is for you to get a fix on what the market and the experts are anticipating from Washington and then to see how treasury prices react to the actual number.

But no consensus is foolproof. For example, Leonard Santow, managing director of Griggs and Santow, New

York City financial consultants specializing in capital markets, tells of a time the nonfarm payroll employment figures were announced, only to be "much weaker than what the market expected." That was good news for investors long in the 30-year T-bond because it rallied immediately. But some investors—those who felt the market was anticipating solid numbers and who were short the long bond—were hurt. As Santow so accurately puts it, "the market has an estimate" on virtually every number, every statistic that affects the bond market. The serious, active investor cannot afford to ignore this fact of life.

But here is the wild card that can cause grief to the casual investor in treasuries, or to the person who does not pay attention. The same sets of statistics released monthly in Washington do not always move or dominate the market every month. In fact, as economic cycles evolve, the market, investors, and the press seem to shift their attention from one set of statistics to another, often without explanation.

Not long ago, the ballooning trade deficit was being heralded as the blasting cap that would reignite inflation. As a result, all eyes and ears were on the merchandise trade deficit announced each month by the Commerce Department. These figures reflected the growing U.S. trade deficit with Japan, dramatically driving home the point that America was buying far more goods from Japan than our big trading partner was buying from us. The trade deficit was seen as a major drain on the strength and worldwide vitality of the U.S. dollar and that had negative connotations for the bond market. As the trade gap began to widen with each announcement, the bond market reacted sharply and treasury prices fell.

Within six months, though, the dollar was a nonstory, the markets were no longer placing that much importance on the trade deficit, the financial press didn't consider it major news, and its impact on bond prices the day that the figures were announced was reduced.

This points to yet another problem facing treasury investors who diligently try to keep informed and to read

46

the market. The U.S. Government securities market is like one big county fair shooting gallery. Wooden ducks crisscross before your eyes on a high speed track. Each duck is an important source of information. But once you've drawn a bead on a plump duck, it disappears from sight.

Yet the fastest, surefire way to lose money in treasuries is not by pouncing on or ignoring every statistic or trend that is perceived to nudge prices in one direction or the other. The death knell is arrogance. When you think the bond market should be reacting one way and it's doing the exact opposite, never fight it. Do an about face and go with the flow.

This is probably the greatest argument of all for setting aside some time during your week to take a good look at bond market behavior regardless of whether your money is in funds or short-term maturities or locked up for the long haul. You want to stay a step ahead.

Remember these principles: The market doesn't react well to good economic news and prices can only go down. The market reacts positively to bad economic news and treasury prices generally always go up. (Unless, of course, market expectations have already anticipated and discounted those moves.) By anticipating the market, you won't get trampled when investors make the wrong call. Because people who have to get out of their positions quickly—whether short or long—will rush to break the door down; the market gyrates. If more people learned how to monitor the news that moves the treasury markets and anticipate how they will react, U.S. Government securities would be an even safer place to be.

16

GOVERNMENT AGENCY BONDS: MORE YIELD, LESS LIQUIDITY

Ask a hundred investors what leaps to mind when you mention U.S. Government securities and you can bet 95 percent will sing out treasury bills, bonds, and notes. Treasuries are clearly the investment of choice for people who want to enjoy rock-solid safety or to speculate on interest rate movements.

One big reason? The Treasury has a powerful public relations machine, known as great word of mouth, working on its behalf. Although some people mistakenly think bank certificates of deposit are the highest yielding, most bulletproof investment of all, the majority of conservative *and* adventurous investors know treasury bills, bonds, and notes are the only securities in the world today that have zero credit risk; they are backed by the full faith and credit of the U.S. Treasury. A bank CD? It is guaranteed only by the Federal Deposit Insurance Corporation, an *agency* of the U.S. Government.

There is a difference, although it's a slight one. Uncle Sam stands behind the obligations of the federal agencies that have been created essentially to make the country function more efficiently. So far, he has never let any agency default on its debts. But "agencies" do not have the ironclad Full Faith and Credit guarantee that makes their word 100 percent worry free.

In years past, investors who could live with a tad more risk have put their money into the coupon securities issued by these federal agencies and have been rewarded handsomely. After all, the Federal Home Loan Bank (FHLB), the Federal National Mortgage Association (FNMA), and the Federal Farm Credit Banks (FFCB), among other agencies, have had to raise money for a variety of reasons, ranging from buying Government-guaranteed mortgages to helping keep farm families solvent. And to convince investors to buy their IOUs instead of credit risk-free T-bills or T-bonds, agencies had to pay a higher coupon yield.

Another reason agencies sold at high premium to treasuries was the bad press they received in the mid-1980s when the Federal Farm Credit Banks were plagued with a rash of bad loans. More recently, a rising tide of thrift industry failures has caused concern over debt instruments issued by the Federal Home Loan Bank. But, again, no one has lost a nickel from a default.

However, agencies have market risk. They behave like any other bond—prices rise when interest rates drop (and vice versa)—and commissions are slightly higher, but there is no fixed level. Most agencies are bought and sold by primary dealers marketing with institutions—pension funds, government bond mutual funds, and other fixed income portfolio managers who want to squeeze every last basis point out of a transaction. Conventional brokers account for only an estimated 15 to 20 percent of the market for agencies today. That's no big surprise. Creditworthiness aside, they are not the same great deal they once were.

Here's why. We're now in the 1990s and the 100-plus basis point premium agencies once enjoyed over treasuries has shriveled to about 20 points. Agencies no longer deliver a towering yield compared to intermediate and long-term treasuries; investors are not being paid for the risk of leaving a debt instrument guaranteed by the U.S. Treasury in favor of one deemed an "obligation" of the U.S. Government.

Second, the market for agencies does not have the same liquidity as the treasury market. Treasuries are auctioned in $8-billion to $10-billion amounts; agencies are underwritten in lots of $300 million to $400 million and sold by investment banking firms. Hence, with a smaller supply and institutional demand, the spreads between the bid and ask prices available to individual investors are much wider than for treasuries. For example, an on-the-run ten-year treasury note had a spread of $^1/_{32}$ to $^2/_{32}$ between bid and ask at the same time a ten-year Fannie Mae bid/ask spread was $^6/_{32}$ to $^8/_{32}$, or almost four times higher.

Third, although many agencies have the same tax benefits of treasuries with yields being exempt from state and local taxes, others do not. Investors have mistakenly bought agency securities and, after paying state taxes on the coupon interest, netted less than a comparably priced treasury note.

Finally, always look at the bottom line, not the big up-front number. Government bond mutual funds, which are often packed with agencies to beef up the yield, may promise better returns than a pure treasury mutual fund. By subtracting the higher management fee of the government bond fund and adding the tax advantages of the all-treasury mutual fund, the safest route may also be the most profitable.

Bid, ask, and yield quotations on U.S. Government agency issues are found in most daily and financial newspapers. The local and state tax-exempt status of these bonds varies from state to state, so be sure to check with your local tax professional:

Federal Farm Credit Bank
Federal Home Loan Bank
Federal Home Loan Mortgage Corp. (Freddie Mac)
Federal Land Bank
Federal National Mortgage Association (Fannie Mae)
Financial Assistance
Financing Corp.
Government National Mortgage Association (Ginnie
 Mae)
Inter-American Development Bank
Residential Funding Corporation (Refco)
Student Loan Marketing Association (Sallie Mae)
World Bank

17

TREASURY FUTURES: UPPING THE ANTE ON RISK AND REWARD

The word "leverage" is the investment community's term for a world-class balancing act. Imagine supporting a hippopotamus—nose first—on the palm of your hand. Keep it in the air long enough and you'll win accolades and applause. But if the beast suddenly makes the wrong move, you can be crushed.

Financially speaking, leverage is the great multiplier. Use leverage, and you multiply your reward—and your risk.

Treasury futures are, quite possibly, the most highly leveraged investment strategy of all. For $5,000, you can control $1 million worth of treasury bills. That's the equivalent of buying the T-bills with one half of 1 percent down and not having to make payments. But you own nothing. What you purchase is a futures contract—an agreement to buy a $1 million T-bill at a specific price on some future date. The margin payment, that one half of 1 percent, is nothing more than a "good faith" deposit.

Futures contracts generally—and treasury futures specifically—have one king-size advantage over other leveraged investments such as buying stocks and bonds on margin. A margined purchase requires you to pay cash for a percentage of the total price and to borrow money and finance the balance. You then pay interest on the money borrowed, even though you can often write it off as an expense against any profits. But the point is, you are on the hook for the total face value of the investment.

With any futures contract, treasuries included, you do not borrow a dime to buy the contract. The good faith deposit buys nothing except control over a huge block of the commodity you promise to buy at that specific date—in this case the $1 million in T-bills. But, remember, those T-bills are only yours temporarily. And you are responsible for their behavior.

Now here's where the excitement of leverage comes into play. You can buy treasury futures of varying maturities on bills, notes, and bonds, but if you are firmly convinced the rate of inflation is going to decline slowly over the next six months, you probably want to go out long on the yield curve. And there you have a choice. You can either buy $25,000 worth of 30-year T-bonds and pay $25,000 cash. Or you might put the same $25,000 into a T-bond fund that invests in the 30-year. (Why? Because the 30-year T-bond most closely tracks the rate of inflation.) Or, if this were April, you could buy a T-bond futures contract due in June. For a deposit of $2,700, or 2.7 percent, you would control $100,000 worth of the 30-year, paying 9 percent. For a cash outlay of one tenth of what it would cost to buy $25,000 worth of T-bonds, you get four times as many bonds.

Treasury bond futures contracts trade at $1/32$ of a percentage point, commonly called a tick. And the contracts are priced the same as one bond, say $88.30/32. Even if T-bond rates dropped only one tick, and the futures contract price the following day was $88.31, you would make $31.25 for that $1/32$ of a point move. If rates drop a full percentage point, you'd make $1,000. Now, that would be no big deal had you shelled out cash to buy the $100,000 of T-bonds, but since you put up only $2,700 for the contract, you make a 37 percent return on your money in just a few days. That's the magic of leverage—the potential of a huge return for a tiny investment.

But, what rockets up also plummets down. "The flip-side of this huge gain is not so rosy," warns Tim Mulholland, assistant vice president of Discount Corporation of New York Futures, a Chicago futures and options brokerage firm. This may be a drastic but not an extraordinary example; however, if your hunch on interest rates is wrong and the long bond price moves down a point over a couple of days, you would lose $1,000 or 37 percent of your equity—the cash deposit you put up on that contract. Worse yet, after dropping $1,000, you would have only $1,700 left, and futures exchange regulations require you to keep $2,000 on margin, so you would get a call to come up with another $300 within 24 hours.

This is not even a severe scenario, according to Mulholland. The 30-year T-bond perched out there on the end of the yield curve, as emphasized all along, is extremely volatile. So it is no surprise that a futures contract of $100,000 in 30-year T-bonds would experience the same sharp swings on very good and very bad news. In an extreme case, theorizes Mulholland, you could have $10,000 in cash supporting a T-bond futures contract and devastating news—war in the Middle East that sends oil to $40 a barrel, coupled with a massive auction of new long bonds—could knock nine points off the price of the T-bonds you own. That's a $9,000 loss in a matter of days. You would get a call for another $1,000 to bring you back to the $2,000 required deposit, but here's a case where you shouldn't answer the call.

First, to lose $9,000 means that both you and your broker were asleep at the switch. A skilled bond broker should have realized that scores of technical indicators were flashing red. The volatile mixture of Middle East tensions and oil are signals enough. Plus, futures exchanges have limits on how far up or down a contract price can move in any given day. With T-bond contracts, the limit is three points up or down in any one trading day. Hence, to lose nine points—and 90 percent of your cash deposit—means that your contracts were "down the limit" three days straight.

18

LIMITING RISK WITH FUTURES

The most fundamental strategy in treasury futures is to build a floor to limit your downside risk before even thinking about going through the roof. On highly leveraged investments, it's human nature—call it optimism or, better yet, greed—to think that even if you're only a little bit right, a small amount of cash can produce mammoth returns.

That's looking down the wrong end of the gun barrel. Instead, make sure your bond broker has studied the technical charts and can tell you where bond prices have hit support levels on interest rate hikes in the past. There is no guarantee that history will repeat itself exactly, but this intelligence can help you and your broker set your stop losses. Stop losses are price levels that you and your broker set up as circuit breakers of sorts. If your futures contract falls to that preset level, it automatically trips that circuit breaker and your position is liquidated.

"With the tremendous leverage in treasury futures, only buy a contract after you know where the price support levels are so you can set your stop loss," advises Tim Mulholland of Discount Corporation of New York Futures. "To minimize risk and maximize return, you must know when to say you are wrong." The wisest way? To limit your downside, pick a point where you'll feel the pain, and don't think in terms of points that cost $1,000. Say to yourself, "I'll risk eight ticks [8/32 of one price point or $250] to make one or two full points [$1,000 or $2,000]."

Actually, this can be accomplished in a variety of ways. While a market order can be a buy or sell order at the current price, a stop order is an order to sell when the price hits a certain level. (A limit order is another way to trigger a buy or sell when the price hits a particular point, while a day order can automatically trigger a buy or sell if the price hits a particular point on a given trading day.) When you figure that prices on treasury futures contracts can fluctuate in seconds, you can see how important it is to stay on top of these markets.

Success in treasury futures involves more than having interest rates move in your favor. For openers, understand that futures are a speculation, not an investment. You do not hold the contract until the expiration date, unlike holding a bill or note to maturity. This would mean you are obligated to take what is called "physical delivery" of the T-bonds (or the bills or notes) and come up with the cash to pay for the full face amount of the contract. Usually, though, you sell out of the contract, hopefully at a profit, before it comes due. But you must also be able to stomach a loss and still sleep at night. Most brokerages would ideally like you to open a treasury futures account with $10,000 cash even though the deposit is only $2,700 for a T-bond contract. They would like to see this cash cushion because they know repeated margin calls may scare you out of the market. The only real rule of thumb—although it's a whiskered bromide— is "if it hurts you to lose or crimps your lifestyle, or both, don't risk your money."

Next, and I've said this over and over, you absolutely must have a firm conviction on which way interest rates and the economy are moving and it doesn't always have to be bullish. Just as you can go short on individual treasuries if you think interest rates will rise and bond prices will fall, you can also go short on a treasury futures contract. But to have no opinion on the domestic markets and the economy or the world at large is a surefire recipe for disaster. The only thing worse is to try and buck the trend. If you get "stopped out" more than one day and you're looking—indeed, praying—for a turnaround, you can bet those prayers will not be answered. Take your losses, and next time, set up a stop loss that automatically takes you out before it costs you too much money.

Professional futures managers never risk more than 5 percent of their cash equity on any one trade.

Probably the best advice you can get on treasury futures is offered by Morris Markovitz, publisher of the *Mercury Market Letter* in New York City and an economic consultant on the futures market: "Keep it simple." Realize that the size of the margin deposit is "no guarantee of performance and has no relationship to price volatility." Furthermore, according to Markovitz, the "more time and study you invest in treasury futures, the better you'll be paid for it." Indeed, that's a rather clever way of stating the most fundamental of truths. And the dreaded flipside is just as valid. Put up your money and do no homework, and you'll pay the price—a big one.

Where do you go to study treasuries futures? You can start with the major commodity exchanges. The Chicago Board of Trade (CBT) trades T-note and T-bond contracts. The Chicago International Money Market (IMM) trades T-bill contracts. Other exchanges trade small contracts of assorted treasury futures, and all will send you extensive trading information. Overseas, T-bond futures contracts trade on the Sydney Futures Exchange, the Singapore International Monetary Exchange, and the London International Futures Exchange.

Different exchanges have different contract sizes, minimum movements, and trading hours. But don't worry about the technicalities. If you're going to up the risk/reward ante by going into treasury futures, make sure you have a skilled, seasoned futures broker, not some boiler-room operator who cold calls, promising immense returns. There are plenty of those characters around, and they have plucked many a pigeon.

Instead, find a pro who will stay with you every step of the way.

19

OPTIONS ON TREASURY FUTURES: WELCOME TO THE CASINO

If treasury futures move too quickly for you—and owning the individual T-bond or T-note does not provide you with the multiplying power of leverage—you have an option. Literally. You can buy or sell puts and calls on treasury futures and limit your exposure to huge losses if interest rates move suddenly and sharply against you. Welcome to the options casino.

Now options, specifically puts and calls, can be quite confusing to first-time speculators. But let's clear the air. Options can be bought and sold on stocks, commodities, and treasuries. These are called "physicals," but options on the actual treasury security are not that liquid and should be avoided. The buying and selling of options on treasury futures contracts is a far more active and liquid market.

That's right. Options on treasury futures are a form of gambling, and you should only "play" if you are firmly convinced that interest rates will move one way or the other. No opinion or no time to formulate one? Steer clear of options, no matter how passionately your broker tries to interest you in them.

Treasury futures options, like any game, have their own ground rules and jargon. For starters, although they are traded in a secondary market—you can buy or sell them through your broker—they carry no guarantee that protects your principal. Indeed, if you buy options on treasury futures—either a put or a call—"you are likely to lose 100 percent of your money three out of four times," warns Robert Prince, manager of research and trading for Bridgewater Associates, a global fixed income and currency management firm in Wilton, Connecticut, "and make a decent amount of money one of four times. It's like putting money in a slot machine." Except that with a slot machine, you simply stuff in the money and pull the handle. Options require strategy.

A call option is a right, but not an obligation, to buy a treasury futures contract (the $100,000 T-bond contract traded on the Chicago Board of Trade, for instance) at a predetermined price, called the striking or exercise price, at a predetermined date, called the expiration date. The cost to buy the option is called a premium. You would only buy a call if you thought interest rates would drop before the expiration date.

The opposite of a call option is a put. This is a way to bet that interest rates will climb and bond prices will fall and can be used as a vehicle to short a treasury futures contract. Buy a put option and you get the right, but not the obligation, to sell the contract at a specific strike price on or before a specific future date. Buying puts is a bearish strategy, so before you place that bet, you should have a keen sense that interest rates will soon move up.

"Essentially, you are buying insurance that interest rates will move in the direction you're anticipating," says Norm Zadeh, who manages the annual U.S. Trading Championships. He, too, contends option writers or sellers have the upper hand in puts and calls because they have factored their risk into the price of the premium.

But if you make a wrong call on interest rate movements, you're not hurt as badly as you would be if you were speculating on the treasury futures contract itself. By owning a call or a put option, you simply do not exercise it and let it expire. You lose only the premium, which is the price you paid for the option in the first place. (Option prices on treasury futures are quoted daily in most newspapers.) Premiums can range from a few 64ths ($1/64$ is equal to $15.62½$) up to $5,000 plus a flat commission of usually $10. But that's all you can lose, while there is no ceiling on how much you can win.

However, you do not lose 100 percent of your call/put option premium at the expiration date. As a "wasting asset," it loses value every day you hold it and do not exercise it. But you also have, pardon the expression, another option. If you realize you made a mistake and sense interest rates will move against you—up instead of down—you simply sell the call back into the options market. Naturally, if you hold it for even a day or two, you won't recover the full amount of your premium, but you won't lose the lion's share of it, either.

The only other way you can lose most or all of the premium is when interest rates do not move at all during the time you own your call. Why? Because the value wastes away while you wait to see some movement in rates, and it expires worthless. The majority of options do, in fact, expire worthless, accounting for the high percentage of losers.

Who is selling the call/put option you are buying? It may be an individual investor, but usually it's an institution. As the "option writer," the seller is betting either that interest rates will not budge or will move against you, the buyer. It's the seller who collects your premium and earns interest on it while you sweat until rates move or the option expires. Think of the seller as the casino; you, the buyer, are the gambler betting against the house. Sure, chances are very slim that you'll hit a jackpot— rates will drop or rise sharply, and you'll exercise your option to pocket a handsome profit by controlling the underlying treasury futures contract. But sometimes the casino loses, too.

Just don't bet on it. "The average person has no hope of winning," says Bruce Babcock, editor and publisher of *Commodity Traders Consumer Report* newsletter. "You know the odds are against you but, as a buyer, you never know how really big the odds are."

20

THE VIEW FROM ABROAD

"An investor in U.S. securities who is not following what is happening around the world," says Carl Weinberg, former chief international economist for Shearson Lehman, "is only playing with half a deck."

Weinberg, now chief economist with High Frequency Economics, a New York City economic advisory firm, knows that major financial institutions have a voracious appetite for instant information to help deal themselves a winning investment hand.

Ironically, Weinberg says there are "no hard and fast rules for cross-border investing" in U.S. Government securities. On the same transaction, while one sophisticated investor may hedge the currency risk and stand only the market risk, another equally skillful investor will not hedge at all.

In Japan, for instance, there are two types of investors in U.S. Government securities—and both stay primarily with the volatile 30-year T-bond. "The first is a pure speculator, a gambler," says John McGivney, a Tokyo-based trader with the U.S. brokerage firm of Smith Barney. Specifically, these are "capital gains traders and not yield or dividend investors," he stresses. "They're constantly looking for an edge." They go long (buy) or go short (sell) the 30-year T-bond precisely for its volatility, knowing that good news, bad news, or any news will move the price and produce a profit depending on their position.

The other Japanese investor in U.S. Governments, according to McGivney, is the "purely passive, long-termer who buys and holds 30-year bonds for 30 years. The two will never meet." Indeed, both are important to the U.S. Government market. The speculators add liquidity to the market, while buy-and-hold investors add stability.

Craig Messinger, an executive with Lehman Brothers International who works in both London and Tokyo, says the Japanese usually buy "when the dollar has bottomed out" against the yen. Messinger's view adds to the consensus that Japanese investors watch our currency exchange rates more than our interest rates.

Nigel Blanshard, a portfolio manager for Century Asset Management in London suggests investors "think of the world as being made up of 15 interest rate markets, all independent economies with their own national problems and characteristics. The English, for instance, have an inflation mentality that is tremendously difficult to suppress." A segment of the Japanese investment community has a speculative, rumor-driven mentality.

The Taiwan Chinese who invest in U.S. Government securities are principally short-term investors who buy and hold treasury bills, often three-month maturities or up to two-year treasury notes, according to Ed Lew, Treasurer with China Trust Bank in New York. They do not buy treasuries for higher interest rates or safety of capital because Taiwan's short-term government note and bank rates are two to three percentage points higher than those of the U.S. Government. Instead, they watch the foreign exchange or "forex" market. The dollar's relationship to other major currencies is a critical signpost that must be watched by U.S. investors because it's a tipoff to capital flows.

For example, if Taiwanese expect the U.S. dollar to appreciate against the NT (New Taiwan) dollar, they will sell NT dollars and buy three-month T-bills. When the bills mature, they will collect the principal and interest and repurchase NT dollars. Remember, their original investment buys more NT dollars than it did three months ago. Again, they are betting on the currency yet, by investing in three-month T-bills, do not have to worry about interest rate risk.

"A lot of overseas investments are based on family

considerations," says Lew. "Here, Chinese *do* want safety in one-year T-bills or two-year T-notes because the proceeds are going for a child's college education or a U.S. residence. They gamble at home in their own markets. Here, they want safety and diversification."

Chinese do not like mutual funds or managed accounts though. Says Lew, "Typically, they like to control their money and make their own decisions. They don't even mind losing as long as they have control."

The main barometer foreign investors watch is the health of the dollar. Severe dollar weakness draws money out of U.S. Government securities; a strong dollar attracts foreign capital. When the dollar is strong and foreign capital flows into short-term treasuries, outsiders are placing a bet on the currency, not on the price of T-bills or T-notes, so it's not necessarily a buy signal for Americans.

Other ways to read the currency barometer: If foreign investors face high short-term interest rates at home and a weak U.S. dollar, their capital will stay put. If U.S. long bond interest rates are declining (bullish) but the U.S. dollar is weak (bearish), foreign capital is caught in a tug-of-war and usually does nothing. But if foreigners see a strong U.S. long bond market (with declining rates) and a brawny dollar, they will line up at the door to buy our government debt.

21

TAXES AND TREASURIES: IT'S NET, NOT YIELD, THAT COUNTS

For investors, there is a single truth to always remember: It's not how much you make but how much you keep that really counts.

Taxes are a fact of life, one of the two "sure things" in this world, and depending on where you live, they can take some voracious bites out of your gross income. We've stressed that many investors never consider the risk consequences they face in chasing the promise of high yield. The same can be said of tax consequences.

Investors in treasuries and other U.S. Government bonds, for example, enjoy some terrific tax advantages but few people really take the time to understand the exemptions they do and do not receive. Fundamentally, interest income earned in owning treasury bills, bonds, and notes is exempt from state and local income tax. However, that same interest is subject to federal income tax. Furthermore, any gains in the value of the treasury that are realized while you hold the instrument are subject to federal, state, and local taxes. This includes any capital appreciation you make in a treasury or government bond mutual fund.

A good rule to remember is that under current tax law, all gains or market profits realized from any stock, bond, or commodity are taxed as income at the federal and state levels. Uncle Sam and all 50 of the state and local tax collectors are not about to subsidize any part of your success in timing investment market moves. At the same time, though, they are willing to grant tax exemptions on the *income* you earn from investing in *their* debt. Consider it a "thank you" for loaning them money as an incentive to keep you reinvesting in their various securities.

However, apart from the fact that interest income from treasury bills, notes, and bonds is exempt from state and local taxes, it is impossible to make a similar blanket statement on other U.S. Government securities. "Many agency debt instruments are exempt from state and local taxes but not all are," warns CPA Chuck Rosenblatt, a tax partner with the Los Angeles accounting firm of Roth, Bookstein & Zaslow. To make matters more confusing, some state tax courts have overturned their previous rulings and levied taxes on income from agency bonds that, in other states, remain tax exempt.

Before you consider an investment in any government security, ask your tax professional for advice on the tax implications.

Indeed, these considerations can be daunting for government bond investors. Investors in mutual funds that hold a mix of treasury and agency bonds may find their monthly income is not state tax-free as it would be if the fund were 100 percent invested in treasuries. Many all-bond mutual funds add corporate, Ginnie Mae, or Fannie Mae bonds to their portfolio to boost yields. "You may even lose the state tax exemption on the portion of the income attributable to the treasuries," says Rosenblatt. Again, check with your tax professional or with tax officials in the state where you reside.

Municipal bonds are the only debt instruments where the interest income is normally exempt from federal taxes. Income from munis is also exempt from state and local taxes. Subtract any fees or commissions and you get an accurate idea of what goes in your pocket.

In fact, accountants urge government bond investors to always look for the net return when evaluating investment alternatives. "Look at the yield after all taxes are paid because that's the one that counts," cautions Jack Benadon, a principal with the Los Angeles certified public accounting firm of Meyer, Benadon, Shapiro. Municipal bond investors who don't want to worry about managing and monitoring should look for a single-state muni bond fund holding only obligations issued by their state of residence in order to get the double tax-free benefits of federal and state exemption.

Although a little shopping can solve that problem, investors face a bigger shock in discovering that the interest from a municipal bond is not always tax-free and could cost them 21 percent in taxes. "Not all muni bonds are alike," warns Benadon. "Some, like private activity municipal bonds, are subject to the Alternative Minimum Tax computation and while you think you are buying a tax-free investment, you are unwittingly not." How do you protect yourself? Insist that your bond broker check with the issuing agency to determine if the interest income from the muni bond you're buying is indeed a "preference item" for computing the AMT.

Buying municipals for their tax benefit may not always be as wise as it seems. Depending on your tax bracket and prevailing interest rates, a partly tax-free treasury or government bond may offer a high, safe yield that delivers a better net-after-tax return. Study all advantages, shortcomings, and alternatives in an investment before you commit your money.

During the 1980s, a number of tax-advantaged investment strategies were eliminated by a spate of tax reform legislation. Today, investors should make sure an investment has a reasonable chance to return a reasonable profit, instead of acting simply as a tax shield. However, some taxwise strategies remain. If you are having an exceptionally good year and you would like to defer income to the next year, you can buy a six-month T-bill maturing in the next calendar year. However, only consider this if you are firmly convinced Congress will not raise federal income taxes within the next 12 months.

Even when you invest in instruments as creditworthy as treasuries and other U.S. Government obligations, it is particularly wise today to huddle with both your broker and your tax professional.

22

MUNICIPAL BONDS: TAX-FREE BUT NOT RISK-FREE

Municipal bonds, commonly called "munis," have a glamorous mystique about them. Many investors think of them as a surefire, risk-free, tax shelter for the wealthy.

No way. Munis are government bonds with some very definite tax advantages, but they have the same market risk as treasuries plus the credit risk of corporate bonds. Indeed, they are kissing cousins to U.S. Government securities but with some very important differences.

First, the interest you earn on a muni is free of federal income tax. Furthermore, if you buy bonds issued in the state where you live, they can be free of state and local income tax. Treasury bond income is exempt only from state and local taxes.

Second—and this is critical—municipal bonds are not risk-free. Investors in munis, unlike investors in treasuries, don't have the peace of mind in knowing the full faith and credit of the United States stands behind the debt. A few muni bonds, like corporate bonds, can default and you can lose your principal as well as your interest.

Third, munis are tough to track. Prices and yields for individual bonds are not quoted in newspapers and only a broker can provide a bid or ask price. And while T-bonds sell in $1,000 face value increments, muni bonds come in lots of $5,000. However, they are price-quoted for comparison in $1,000 denominations.

But there are two major similarities between municipals and U.S. Governments. Muni bond prices rise when interest rates drop and fall when rates climb. In short, they react to changes in monetary policy or inflation and behave as any other bonds do. A 30-year muni is just as volatile as a 30-year T-bond. And like treasuries, munis pay interest semiannually.

Specifically, though, what are municipal bonds? They are debt securities or obligations sold either by a state, to finance day-to-day governmental operations, or by a municipality—a city or township—usually to raise money for a project benefiting local residents. Again, unlike treasuries, you cannot buy them direct from the issuer. Individual munis are sold only through brokerage firms, or as shares in a municipal bond mutual fund.

The bottom line: When you invest in a muni, you're loaning out your money to your state or city government in exchange for a promised repayment on a certain date plus a fixed rate of interest.

Maturities for munis can range from one week to 30 years, so you can use them to meet specific investment goals. Before you choose tax-free bonds over taxable bonds, though, calculate the "tax equivalent yield." This is the percentage you would earn if you were paying federal taxes on the muni bond income. The "tax equivalent yield" is often greater than the taxable yield on U.S. Governments or even corporate bonds. For instance, assuming you are in the 28 percent federal income tax bracket, you would need to purchase a treasury bond yielding 11.11 percent to equal the tax equivalent yield on a muni yielding 8 percent.

Munis are not just a smart investment for the wealthy; they're attractive if you're in the basic 28 percent federal income tax bracket and want to avoid additional taxable income. But, frankly, there is an art to investing in munis, and Key 23 will explain how to master it.

23

THE ART OF
INVESTING IN MUNIS

For starters, munis come in several forms. The most preferable are state "government obligation" or GO bonds. Approved by the legislature, issued and backed by the state's treasury, GOs are also redeemed by the state treasurer at maturity. The other version is a "municipal revenue bond," usually issued by a city to finance a public works project. Projects may range from a new sewer system to a bridge or a domed stadium, but the bonds are repaid by the revenues collected from the citizenry. Now we're talking risk. Revenue bonds can default if the project is an operational failure and doesn't generate enough cash to make the interest payments or to pay off the bonds at maturity.

How can you protect yourself against muni bond defaults? In several ways. Munis, like corporate bonds, are rated for creditworthiness by the two main business credit rating services: Dun and Bradstreet and Moody's. The rating reflects the underlying strength of the issuer and its ability to redeem the bond at maturity. The safest munis are rated AAA, and anything below an A rating can be chancy. Munis with B and C ratings usually carry a little higher yield but much, much more risk; they're true *junk bonds*.

Never buy any municipal bond rated lower than an A and never buy a high yield or junk muni, unless you are willing to assume the credit risk. In the past, you had as much as a two-point or greater spread between yields on junkers and high quality munis. In recent years, it has been only three quarters of one point, so why take the risk?

Here are some other red flags. Never trade munis

unless you want to make your broker rich and yourself poor. With munis, you should hold to maturity unless you have to liquidate. Why? The secondary market for municipals isn't as liquid as the Treasury markets and you could lose 10 to 15 percent of your original investment if you liquidate when interest rates are rising.

Other red flags: Steer clear of revenue bonds issued to build and operate hospitals and nursing homes; they frequently default if the medical care facility is poorly managed. Beware when a salesperson calls and asks for an investment decision on a muni bond "immediately," as if you are going to lose out on a priceless opportunity. Not true.

Zero munis can be great tools for planning for retirement or educational needs or for readying a lump sum for a balloon payment at a designated future date. But there are key points to remember and specific questions that savvy investors will bring to the table before adding zeros to their portfolio.

Zero munis are even less liquid than the general muni market since most investors buy these bonds for the purposes listed above—long-range planning—and they hold to maturity rather than actively trade them. Since zero munis have been in great demand of late, they tend to trade at lower yields (higher prices) than comparable couponed munis. And, don't forget, because of these lower yields and no current income stream, zero munis can be quite volatile, subject to wide swings in interest rates as well as investor sentiment.

If you want to lock in a guaranteed rate of return in your zero muni portfolio, make sure the bonds you buy are noncallable and of the best credit quality. If you buy callable bonds and your yield at the time of purchase is below that call level, you should see all sorts of red flags waving. What could happen? If rates drop, and the bond is called at that higher yield (lower price), you could actually lose money. In fact, this is one of the few scenarios where investors don't make a profit in the face of falling rates.

And remember, depending on where you live, muni

yields in some states do not walk in lockstep with swings in interest rates and the treasury market. For example, bonds from California, New York, and Massachusetts come with a premium because of the high taxes levied in those states. As expected, states with no tax—such as Texas and Nevada—sell at a discount. Your broker should be able to help you get your hands on a copy of the "blue list" showing all munis currently outstanding, by state, both zeros and couponed bonds.

Another tip: In bear markets for stocks, brokerages try to sell packaged municipal bond investments as "safe havens." Some are called "municipal bond unit trusts," but they often hold low quality bonds with higher yields and heavy sales fees. Smart idea: Shop four or five brokerages for the best quote on a high quality individual muni and shop hard. Fees, commissions, and markups vary, and the muni market is the least fairly priced of all the fixed income markets.

There are plenty of green flags to help you make a wise buy. Look for high-yielding bonds with what are called "credit enhancements." This could be either municipal bond insurance that the issuer, not the investor, buys. Or for the ultimate in safety, where the muni is escrowed to maturity with treasury securities. This covers you in two ways: First, if the municipality defaults on the bond, the treasury continues to pass the income stream to you on a tax-free basis; second, this is as close as you come in the muni market to owning the equivalent of a solid T-bond.

Meanwhile, here are some specific muni bond investment strategies. Consider a "laddered portfolio" of maturities: a combination of three-, five-, seven- and ten-year bonds to diversify interest rate risk and keep a steady income stream flowing. Plus, stay away from long-term munis unless the yield differential is significantly higher than that for intermediate maturities. For example, buy a 30-year muni only if it is yielding a minimum of 1.5 percent more than seven- to ten-year munis. But above all, make sure it has an A rating or higher and that you can hold it to maturity.

24

SAVINGS BONDS: A SAFE AND SHREWD INVESTMENT

It's almost an American tradition to buy a U.S. savings bond for a newborn. After all, these bonds are the one baby gift youngsters never outgrow. They are inexpensive and sell at a 50 percent discount from their face value: a $50 bond costs $25. Or you can buy $30,000 worth, the maximum amount of bonds in any one year, for $15,000, and you pay no commissions, fees, or mark-ups on your investment.

Savings bonds, like all treasuries, are rock-solid safe, backed by the full faith and credit of the U.S. Government. They may not pay the highest yield available in the fixed income market, but the interest rate is adjusted periodically to make them competitive. They are easy to buy; most banks sell them and companies offer Bond-a-Month payroll deduction purchasing plans for pain-free accumulation. What's more, you don't have to watch these bonds like a hawk because there is no secondary market and, hence, no price fluctuation. Just put them in a safe place, sleep tight, and forget about them until they mature.

If savings bonds are such trouble-free investments, why don't they get better press? Why do brokers, financial planners, and other investment advisors treat them like Cinderellas, trotting them out only when a nagging client demands to know more about them?

The reality is Uncle Sam does not have a legion of public relations powerhouses pitching its investment wares. At one point, the U.S. Treasury had promotion managers in every city calling on editors and, essentially, beating the drums for savings bonds. But no longer. The Treasury Department, like other federal agencies and nonprofits, has to rely on donated advertising space to get its message out. And brokers and other financial service salespeople rarely, if ever, recommend savings bonds because, quite frankly, there's no economic incentive; no one makes a commission selling a savings bond.

Yet, taking a close look at savings bonds is wise for any investor. First, they're affordable. As mentioned above, the Series EE bonds sell at a 50 percent discount or half of their face value. All savings bonds, regardless of size, automatically mature in 12 years, but they can be redeemed earlier if you need the cash. I would cash in my savings bonds—and I buy the maximum allowed by law every year—only if the wolf were at the door. They should be held to maturity.

Second, savings bonds have an investment "floor." Federal law guarantees the U.S. Treasury will pay you interest of at least 6 percent a year until maturity. However, you could earn more. The effective interest rate, set every May 1 and November 1, is 85 percent of the average market interest rate paid the prior six months on five-year treasury notes. And you could earn less than 6 percent a year, too, but only if you redeem them before five full years. Cash out earlier, and interest paid ranges from 4.27 percent in the first year to 5.50 percent in the fourth year. Still, there is no ceiling to the yield; as T-notes climb, so do savings bonds.

These bonds have an extra attraction: The interest income earned is exempt from state and local taxes.

25

SAVINGS BONDS: A TAX-WISE WAY TO PAY FOR COLLEGE

Once simply a stodgy way to save, U.S. savings bonds now sport some additional, stylish tax advantages. Section 135 of the IRS Code allows American taxpayers to buy savings bonds for educational purposes for themselves, their spouse, or children. Depending on the purchaser's tax bracket, up to 100 percent of the income is tax-free. The tax exclusion phases out for married taxpayers with incomes between $60,000 and $90,000 and for single taxpayers between $40,000 and $55,000, adjusted for inflation.

This makes savings bonds that have been designated as "education bonds" better performers than tax-free money market funds and at least equal to yields from tax-exempt and considerably riskier municipal bonds, according to Alan Sumutka, an associate professor of accounting at Rider College in Lawrenceville, New Jersey. He once calculated that the 7.81 percent federal tax-free yield of education bonds was equal to a 10.85 percent taxable yield for a taxpayer in the 28 percent bracket. And when the state tax exemption is factored in, the effective yield is even higher.

To get the full interest exclusion, you must be at least 24 years old and designate the savings bonds as being purchased for educational purposes. That doesn't mean they can only be used to underwrite the cost of a college or university. Many trade schools and technical training programs qualify for the break. But the "educational bonds" with the full exclusion cannot be bought in a child's name.

Instead, for a partial exclusion and a little more flexibility, you can buy the bonds in the child's name, make the youngster the owner, list his or her social security number and give yours as the beneficiary. Because savings bond interest accrues as unearned income, you have to file only one income tax return, called an "intent return," for the first year. Afterward, you just list the amount of unearned income the child accrues, and as long as it is less than $500 per year, the IRS writes it off that year and every year thereafter. Plus, you do not have to file subsequent tax returns for the child.

On the other hand, if you are in the 28 percent tax bracket and buying large amounts of savings bonds, you can, again by law, defer reporting the interest income until you cash them in to pay the first year tuition. As a result of the 1986 Tax Reform Act, interest earned by a child under age 14 is taxed at the parents' tax rate. After age 14, the interest is taxed at the child's obviously lower rate. Nevertheless, in most cases, all federal taxes on savings bonds yields are deferred until maturity.

What happens if the Series EE bonds mature and you don't want to take the proceeds? You can exchange them for Series HH savings bonds (minimum investment $500) and keep earning for another ten years. This time, though, you will receive interest payments twice a year, and that income is subject to federal taxes. HH bonds are not covered by the Section 135 interest exclusion, but they are exempt from state and local taxes.

Banks and savings and loan associations sell savings bonds. Fill out an application, pay your money, and the financial institution will mail them to you in one to two weeks.

Redemption is immediate. Series EE savings bonds can be redeemed without any fees or administrative charges at most banks or savings institutions that sell them. Series HH bonds can be redeemed only at Federal Reserve Banks or their branches. It's wise not to let savings bonds linger long past their maturity dates. Lost or damaged bonds are replaced free. But, if you make a claim on a savings bond six years after its maturity date, you have to furnish the serial numbers. It can be a hassle.

26

MUTUAL FUNDS: WHERE WALL STREET CROSSES MAIN STREET

Robert Fleming had the germ of a brilliant idea when he invented the forerunner to the modern-day mutual fund in Scotland back in 1873. Round up small amounts of money from many investors, pool it in a single pot, hire an expert to monitor the investment eight hours a day and make the tough decisions on when to buy and sell, then split the profits. Or share the losses.

The philosophy of mutual fund investing hasn't changed in the last 120 years. Investors share the rewards and the risks. They have a small stake in dozens, maybe hundreds, of different investments they could never afford to buy on their own. None of their personal time and angst is spent poring over prospectuses, battling with brokers, worrying over whether they should buy, sell, or stay put. And while fund investors will never slug a bases-loaded grand slam homer and parlay a $2 stock into a $200 a share megawinner, they won't strike out shooting for the moon at the exact moment the market plunges or when that hot stock suddenly turns cold. They float when individual investors freefall.

Mutual funds offer this same bushelbasket of benefits to people investing in U.S. Government securities: Your money is spread across a range of maturities and yields; your money is watchdogged by a pro with the experience, expertise, research tools, and market savvy to make skillful, emotion-free, strategic buy and sell decisions; you enjoy safety in numbers as you share any interest rate jolts with your fellow fundholders.

Plus, there is one other king-sized advantage that investors in government bond funds have over people who invest on their own: clout. Your portfolio manager has the buying power and the connections to execute a trade at the best price and institutional commission rates—a wafer-thin $1/256$ of a point—instead of the one to five full percentage points you would pay as a retail customer buying and selling in small lots. As Burt Berry, publisher and owner of *NoLoad FundX,* a monthly mutual fund newsletter, so graphically puts it: "When you buy $10,000 in treasuries from your stockbroker, you just have access to his inventory. It's like buying a used car. When you go to sell it back to him, he has 100 models just like yours all driven by little old ladies. You can imagine the price he'll give you for your ten bonds."

Yet, there is one giant drawback, too. Diversification has always been a big selling point among marketeers of equity or stock-based mutual funds. If one or more of the stocks in the portfolio sink, the theory is those price drops will be offset by price gains in other stocks and the mutual fund, as a whole, will not be jolted by a performance laggard. But in a bond fund, whether corporates or governments, a boost in interest rates will hurt every security in the portfolio. They are all fixed income securities and they all fall when rates move up. Conversely, when interest rates drop, the portfolio holdings react en masse and the net asset value (NAV), your price-per-share, posts a gain.

Then there is a prevailing myth about government bond mutual funds that, if allowed to perpetuate, could hurt investors. Specifically, the myth is that government bond funds have greater liquidity than individual treasuries and that when interest rates spike and prices fall, fundholders can sell out at the net asset that day. In truth, the secondary market for treasuries is just as liquid for individual owners as for fundholders. It's just that transaction costs are likely to be lower in a fund if you made sure it was a truly cost-efficient fund before you invested. (See Key 30.)

However, even those efficiencies can be offset by the greater flexibility individual investors enjoy, depending on the circumstances. For example, if bad news erupts suddenly after market hours in the United States and interest rates leap and treasury prices fall, an investor owning treasuries can always instantly sell a position on a bond market somewhere in the world, while the mutual fund investor can call in a sell order but must wait until the U.S. bond market opens before it's executed. The fund portfolio manager rarely works around the clock, but a vigilant bond broker, monitoring client positions, does.

Despite these and other tradeoffs, government bond funds are, in many respects, the Cinderellas of the mutual fund industry. And that's unfair. Sure, mutual funds have been described as "everyman's" (and "everywoman's") investment vehicle, but the spotlight seems to always fall on stock funds. According to *Donoghue's Mutual Funds Almanac,* as we enter the 1990s, there are more than 3,000 mutual funds registered with the Securities and Exchange Commission. An estimated 30 million Americans have more than a trillion dollars invested in mutual funds. However, there are only 133 mutual funds that invest exclusively in U.S. Government bonds and fewer still that hold only treasuries.

Why? Simply put, government bond funds aren't exciting. They aren't sexy. The total return figures will never grab headlines like Fidelity's Magellan, a stock fund that delivered a 1,024 percent return to investors over the last ten years. What's more, investors generally do not understand the inner workings of government bond funds. Nor do they realize that government bond funds can efficiently fill voids in their investment portfolio and, more importantly, can be used to target—and reach—specific investment goals.

27

THE FUNDAMENTALS OF GOVERNMENT BOND FUND INVESTING

A generation ago, investment lore had it that people who bought government bonds only wanted safety and income. Maybe that was true then before the great and sudden popularity of the certificate of deposit. CDs are simple: Sign up and hand over your money for awhile. Today, I find investors who are in shorter-to-intermediate maturity no-load mutual funds want capital appreciation, too.

The problem is, they sometimes over-diversify in bond funds. We've all heard the mantra of spreading the risk to smooth out market fluctuations. That's wise when your pie consists of stocks, bonds, real estate, and cash. But diversifying among, say, three different intermediate U.S. Government funds because you want to pit portfolio managers against each other is a redundant exercise. All three funds will react to interest rate changes almost identically.

However, if you do have a strong sense that interest rates may decline and want to diversify for yield, consider putting 5 to 10 percent of the investible assets and no more in a so-called junk bond fund, perhaps another 15 percent in an A- to AAA-rated corporate bond fund, 60 percent in a short- to intermediate-term government bond fund, and the remaining 5 percent in a 30-year T-bond fund. Remember, you've introduced credit risk to a portion of your portfolio, but you're opening the door for possible higher yields.

Meanwhile, where bonds fall short is in protecting investors from inflation. Sure, you get a stream of income while bonds mature or while you remain in a bond fund, but it's no secret the dollars you walk away with when you cash out will be worth less than the dollars originally invested. To protect yourself against inflation if you're doing retirement planning, consider putting a portion of your assets into three-month or six-month T-bills or a T-bill fund. Treasury bills track inflation very closely. In 1981, when inflation soared to double-digit levels, T-bill yields kept pace.

There are dozens of very fine newsletters and advisory services to help investors select the fund that's right for them. It would be nice to subscribe to a cross section so you could mine and compare the informational nuggets. But there is also a wealth of information in mutual fund prospectuses, the SEC-inspected offering circular provided on request to new investors. Here is what to look for and compare. If any information is missing, check with the fund itself or steer clear:

- Investment objective: Spells out what the fund is trying to achieve and how it invests to reach that goal. A fund, by law, cannot deviate from its stated objectives.
- Net asset value history. Shows NAV growth (or loss) on a quarterly and year-end basis.
- Income and capital gain history by quarters and totals.
- Fees, specifically management fees, loads (front and rear), 12b-1 fees, dividend reinvestment fees.
- Expense ratio: Avoid anything over 2 percent.
- Total return: The crucial performance yardstick.
- Portfolio composition: Percentage of cash, bonds, common stocks, if any.
- Portfolio holdings: What you see is what it owns—amounts, value, maturity, percentage of net assets.
- Average weighted maturity: Gives you an idea of how rate changes will impact the portfolio as a whole.

28

YOUR BOND FUND GOAL: CAPITAL PRESERVATION

Before you invest, make sure the vehicle will get you to your destination, safe and sound. The fact is that government bond funds, like treasuries themselves, are not the right funds for capital growth. Want to build your assets and want to see big numbers? Stick with stock funds and pray you find a talented mutual fund manager.

Instead, government bond funds are designed for investors who want to preserve their capital and generate a monthly income stream. Or investors who want to park money at a yield higher than a bank pays and without freezing the funds in a certificate of deposit. Or who want tax-advantaged yields with rock-solid safety, something municipal bond funds can't deliver.

However, competition for the investor dollar is a lovely incentive to innovate and in the last few years we've seen specialized mutual funds that give investors the same play on bad news and many of the same sophisticated strategies they can get and employ from buying individual governments in the secondary market. A new crop of bond funds lets you target maturities just as if you were buying the treasury itself. Others deliver the same highly leveraged advantages of zeros or stripped coupon treasuries without having to pay hefty commissions.

In short, U.S. Government bond funds today can replicate all of the same advantages of buying individual U.S. Government securities, while eliminating many of the shortcomings. But you must know how to buy them, what to look for, what to avoid. That's right. Not all bond funds are created, structured, and managed equally. They have a bewildering number of different fees, features, investment objectives, performance histories, and total returns. Just as treasury investing is a lot more complicated than it appears to the average buy-and-hold-to-maturity person, you must shop government bond funds diligently until you find one that fits your personality, risk tolerance, and financial objectives like a glove.

The big question, though, before you set off on a shopping trip is whether the time-honored concept of mutual funds really is right for you. Unfortunately, there are no easy answers. It boils down to asking yourself some highly personal questions that really dictate the direction you take as a treasury investor.

First, if you want convenience and you don't mind paying for it, a carefully selected no-load U.S. Government bond fund makes sense. The fund's portfolio managers watch the Fed for you, monitor the market-moving news out of Washington and world financial capitals for you, negotiate with brokers and dealers for the best price and execution, and fashion sophisticated yield-enhancing strategies on your behalf.

Second, if you have only a limited amount of money to commit to the fixed income component of your investment portfolio, a mutual fund may be a wise choice. After all, one treasury bill would cost you $10,000.

Third, if you agonize, freeze, or procrastinate when it comes to making hard buy and sell investment decisions, mutual funds are for you. Portfolio managers are professional decision-makers. Individual investors in treasuries may find themselves in contrarian positions watching friends fleeing with the pack at a time when the market is signalling a buy. There is peer pressure in investing, but if you read the market accurately and don't try to fight it, you'll find it's invariably right.

However, the mutual fund approach to treasury investing might not be right if you have a firm conviction on interest rates and you want to pursue it at every end of the market—short, long, and intermediate. Or if you want the ability and flexibility to try sophisticated strategies like leverage, puts and calls, and futures—in short, if you want to get involved with the market and call your own shots on your own terms. If you want hands-on involvement, team up with a seasoned bond broker and forge a client relationship based on mutual trust and respect.

If you feel more comfortable in a mutual fund, let's go shopping with the pros and find the right one.

29

CHOOSING A GOVERNMENT BOND FUND: ASK THE HARD QUESTIONS

With 133 open-end government bond funds, 20 closed-end bond funds, 262 money market funds, and another 63 mutual funds investing in U.S. agency debt obligations, picking a solid, steady performer that meets your financial goals is no cakewalk.

The mutual fund industry has discovered the investor marketplace is a bare-knuckle free-for-all where investors must be sold, not just informed. The result: cold-calling brokers, full page ads, direct mail blitzes, and siren-song seminars that all but guarantee big profits and promise financial security forever.

Indeed, with 3,000 mutual funds selling their expertise, it isn't surprising that the investor is barraged with seductive statistics and enticing claims. But government bond funds are a breed apart. True, the fundamentals are the same, but bond funds have peculiarities of their own, like modest returns, so their virtues often get lost in the scramble for towering yields.

Let's start with the age-old argument of load versus no-load mutual funds. So-called "load" mutual funds are usually sold by investment brokerages; the load, of course, is a commission shared by the firm, the salesperson, and sometimes a separate selling organization or wholesaler known as the sponsor. The traditional load is stiff—8.5 percent of the cash creamed off the top—so you start off in the hole. Your fund must post a 10 percent return just to recoup your commission and get you out of the red.

The archrival of the load fund is the no-load fund. No-loads started as no-frills alternatives to load funds and have captured investor fancy. Most of the cash invested, in theory (but not always in practice), goes into the portfolio. Investors sign up for no-load funds by mailing a coupon or calling an 800 number. Some of the biggest names in the mutual fund world such as Dreyfus, Fidelity, and Vanguard dropped their loads in the early 1970s when a stock market plunge sent investors scrambling for the safety of banks and other depository investments. But loads and other fees are coming back in fashion.

Lately, a hybrid has emerged—the low-load fund. Low-loads typically charge anywhere from 2 to 4 percent and, again, it's off the top. Some fundwatchers are outraged that one-time no-load funds are collecting even a low load, feeling there is no justification for it. With no sales force to compensate, the commission is going straight into management's coffers.

Do load funds outperform no-load funds? "The presence or absence of a load has nothing to do with fund performance," reports Burt Berry, publisher of the widely respected *NoLoad FundX* newsletter, based in San Francisco. However, he cites a *Wall Street Journal* inquiry into this very question. The investment performance of no-load funds was found to have a "slight edge" over load funds.

Nevertheless, any load, regardless of size, is for obvious reasons a prohibitive expense for anyone investing in U.S. Government bond funds. A spectacular total return in a government bond fund is 11 to 12 percent annually. A stock fund with a hot-handed portfolio manager in a strong year could produce double-digit returns as high as 50 percent a year. Investors reaping that kind of reward might not grumble over paying a one-time 4 to 8 percent sales commission. But anyone investing in a government bond fund will never see huge double-digit returns, so they should think twice about paying a load.

It's a direct drain on total return—the key performance measurement that includes net asset value increases plus capital gains and dividends.

Not all loads are levied up front. Not long ago, some mutual funds imposed what they called a "deferred sales charge." It penalized investors, on a sliding scale, for cashing out of the fund. The first-year charge was 5 percent, second-year was 4 percent and so on, disappearing in the sixth year. Meantime, these same funds, by not charging a front-end sales commission, promoted themselves as no-load or "NL" funds. Fortunately, for investors, the Securities and Exchange Commission cracked down on the practice and forced them to fully disclose and explain the nature of the fees. Nowadays, this is called a "redemption fee." Again, this is a totally unnecessary cost, nothing more than a hind-end load, and any U.S. Government bond fund charging one should be avoided.

Far more common, less expensive, but a rip-off nonetheless, is an expense the Investment Company Institute, the mutual fund industry trade organization, lobbied past the SEC about a decade ago. It's called rule 12b-1, and it allows mutual funds to charge fund investors a fee to cover advertising, marketing, and promotional expenses. The SEC failed to put a ceiling on the fee, but the idea quickly caught on and about half of all mutual funds impose one; the amount ranges from .25 percent to 1.25 percent each year that the investor remains in the fund. View any 12b-1 charge as a red flag and avoid any funds that levy it.

Yet another hidden fee to watch for is a commission for reinvesting dividends into the fund. One of the prime advantages of investing in a mutual fund is the automatic reinvestment feature; you don't have to remember to do it yourself. Dividend reinvestment fees were a customary practice in the 1960s. Some fund managers even charged a fee or commission for investing capital gains, an egregious act if there ever was one.

30

WATCHING FUND EXPENSES

Ferreting out hidden costs and bypassing U.S. Government bond mutual funds that bristle with a variety of charges is absolutely essential. The lower the fees, the greater the return—and that, of course, is especially important in a bond fund where returns are lower to begin with.

Are there benchmarks? Look for a total expense ratio of about 1.25 percent. This is a combination of management, investment advisory, custodial, and legal fees, plus transfer fees and distribution fees divided by the average assets outstanding. The largest component of this is the annual management fee, which should average around .50 or one half of 1 percent of your total investment. This pays for the portfolio manager's time and talent and covers the fund's administrative costs and overhead.

"Expense ratios and sales charges are much, much more important in bond funds than stock funds," stresses John Rekenthaler, senior analyst with Morningstar, Inc., publisher of *Mutual Fund Values,* which closely tracks the internal operations and performance of 1,100 mutual funds, including almost every government and treasury bond fund. He contends that bond portfolio managers are not entitled to a richer fee "because the amount of value the manager can add to your return by making correct decisions is much less than in a common stock fund. The range of returns is narrower."

The best performing all-treasury bond fund one recent year returned 9.2 percent to investors while the "worst performer" in the group produced a 4.8 percent annual return. "By comparison, equity funds were all over the planet," says Rekenthaler. "Some made 30 percent.

Some lost money." Meanwhile, expense ratios for government bond funds in 1989 ranged from 1.68 percent for Kidder Peabody's Government Income Fund, to .35 percent or one third of 1 percent for Vanguard's Spartan Ginnie Mae Fund.

Once you've identified a list of government bond funds with an acceptable expense ratio, whittle the group down to a few that meet your investment goals and have a good track record with high average yields and high total return. Some purists might argue that this is attacking the problem from the wrong direction. The key to performance here is ridding the investment vehicle of excess baggage and then finding a fund that fits.

Locating the right mutual fund starts with the prospectus. By federal law, all mutual funds are investment companies and must file a prospectus with the SEC. The prospectus contains the Investment Objective and what the fund invests in to reach that goal. For example, Federated Government Income Securities, a Pittsburgh-based low-load fund that recently earned a very rare five-star rating and buy recommendation from *Mutual Fund Values,* says it seeks "current income." Translated, its fund manager is looking for maximum yield with low risk. For the most recent year, it yielded 10.2 percent. How? By investing at least 65 percent of its assets into mortgage-backed securities and the balance in treasury notes. *Mutual Fund Values* credits the fund with "astute interest rate calls that have made the fund a top performer in both bull and bear markets."

Now, here's a prime example where it pays to do your homework and be flexible. Federated's Government Income Securities charges a load and has a redemption fee. At first glance, that would scratch it from a list of candidates. But, the one-time load is only 1 percent, not 4 or 8 percent, and the redemption fee is .75 percent in the first year, not 5 percent. Plus, the management fee is just .75 percent for a total expense ratio of .93 percent. On balance, that's a small price to pay for five-star rated performance where the minimum investment is only $1,500.

Nevertheless, although two thirds of the holdings in this Federated fund are not treasury obligations and, therefore, not 100 percent backed by the full faith and credit of the U.S. Treasury, they are U.S. Government agency debt, hence there is very little credit risk. But, there is market risk. With maturities of many of its Ginnie Mae and Fannie Mae securities extending as far as 2019, fundholders get some pretty good jolts on interest rate moves.

The problem here and with any mutual fund is continuity of performance. What happens if the portfolio manager leaves?

Kurt Brouwer, a principal in Brouwer & Janachowski, a San Francisco investment advisory that uses only no-load mutual funds to manage money, says any disruption in portfolio management hierarchy will impact fund performance. It's most dramatic in a stock fund with a winning record. "But too often a government bond portfolio manager is an order taker, especially if he's just buying Fannie Maes. Those people are really in a straitjacket because to keep current yields high, all they can do is go out further on the yield curve."

However, if a government bond fund has delivered good yields and total returns over a two- to three-year period, Brouwer says you can make a toll free phone call to the fund management company and get the name or names of the managers responsible. Then, if performance starts falling below benchmarks, like the Shearson Lehman Intermediate Term Index or the Salomon Brothers Long Bond Index, another free phone call will reveal if that same manager is still at the helm. If not, it may be a signal to sell.

31

BOND FUNDS: FINDING THE BEST DEAL

Investors are too often the new victims of the old shell game. They see a whopping yield in some promotional brochure or ad and visualize the money in their pocket, never asking for proof or the names of other investors.

Mutual fund investors have had their share of disappointments—and hard dollar losses. Enticed by big performance numbers, they are convinced history can repeat itself. You see it mainly in stock funds. The mythical Interplanetary Fund had a 21 percent average rate of return over the last ten years. However, take a close look at Interplanetary and you discover the fund posted big double-digit returns only in its early years. After the portfolio manager was hired away by a competitor, the fund performed miserably in the last few years. To get the big picture, look at each piece.

That is true for U.S. Government bond funds. Investors often chase the highest yield to boost monthly income. Fund managers know that and sometimes take risks, adding longer maturities to the portfolio even though it deviates from the portfolio policy. Here are some tricks of the trade that have bilked unfortunate investors who believed all U.S. Government bond funds are rock solid and risk free.

For example, marketplace interest rates are averaging 8 percent, but a bond fund portfolio manager needs an edge to attract new investors and generate new management fees. He buys high-coupon treasury bonds with a current yield of 12 percent and selling at a premium, $120—or $20 over par. With this fresh injection of high yield, the fund sponsor runs ads proclaiming "Now get 10 percent return annually in U.S. Government-backed fund."

"People stand in line to get these yields but they don't understand the risk," explains Gerald W. Perritt, editor of *The Mutual Fund Letter,* a Chicago-based newsletter. "The shock for investors comes later when the notes and bonds start maturing and are redeemed at par—$100." Fundholders lose at least 20 percent of their principal. To protect yourself, ask the fund salesperson or customer service representative for an estimate on the "total return," not just "current yield." Then ask if the portfolio manager sticks with the fund's objectives as stated in the prospectus or does he have the freedom to experiment to pump up the yield. If you don't get a straight, clear answer, stay away.

So-called Ginnie Mae bond funds often trumpet yields two to three percentage points over the returns of all treasury funds but they can be treacherous. These are government *agency* bonds issued—and backed—by the Government National Mortgage Association and not by the U.S. Treasury. Specifically, these bonds are clusters of home mortgages, originally underwritten by a savings and loan or other home lender and sold for cash to GNMA which, in turn, resells them to investors. They pay a high yield because they often have maturities as long as the 30-year T-bond and are as volatile as that T-bond, too. When interest rates climb, Ginnie Mae bond prices drop sharply and fund investors lose principal.

But here's the rub. When rates drop, homeowners tend to refinance their houses and the underlying mortgages are often paid off or called, frequently at no profit to the holder. For investors lured into the fund by the rich yield, it's a little like heads, you lose, tails, you lose or break even.

Nevertheless, other mutual fund managers will write call options on bonds held in their portfolios to pump up yields and, hence, monthly income. This is a side contract giving an outside investor the right to purchase the bond at a certain price within a specific time in exchange for a cash payment called a premium. The portfolio manager writing the option bets interest rates won't move beyond a certain range. Thus the option won't be exercised, will expire worthless, and the fund earns the premium as a capital gain.

However, even though the option-writing practice is fully disclosed in the fund prospectus and investment objectives, there is a big risk to fundholders. If interest rates do drop and the bond price rises to what's called a striking price, the option holder can call the bond away and the mutual fund investor doesn't participate in the profit. And if interest rates rise, call option writing doesn't protect the fundholder from more than a modest price loss, so the net asset value tumbles.

"Investors are getting wary of all the call options written on government bond funds," says John Rekenthaler, the senior analyst with Morningstar, Inc. "In theory, short-term gains are distributed to shareholders along with any other income received by the fund to boost the apparent yield." He feels this practice, although legal, is risky deception at best. "Technically, short-term capital gains are not a true component of yield, while call options are very damaging to a mutual fund's long-term total return," contends Rekenthaler.

32

BOND FUNDS: FREE CANAPÉS AND COSTLY LUNCHES

If some U.S. Government bond mutual fund managers resort to risky ploys to raise yields and win new investors, other managers pare their expense ratios to beef up the all-important profit barometer—total return. How? New-to-the-market mutual funds will waive the management fee as a promotional ploy to lower expenses and bring in investors. Then once the portfolio is plump with dollars, the management fee inevitably appears.

Mutual fund marketing experts know from experience that investors will rarely bail out unless horrendous performance or a disastrous market eats deeply into capital, and holders flee for survival. Caveat: The canapés are often free but the lunch isn't. Funds that waive management fees often require large initial investments and will limit withdrawals to a certain amount. Obviously, these strategies are designed to build up the fund as quickly as possible. Plus, a waived management fee is just that— waived temporarily. It's likely to reappear, so expect it. In the meantime, keep your eye on the fund's bottom line—total return.

Conventional wisdom in mutual funds holds that it's wise to join a fund family like Kemper, Fidelity, or Vanguard so you can re-allocate your assets easily and quickly with a telephone call. In theory, that's a brilliant concept. Just make sure you are not charged a switching fee for moving money.

Few people actually change funds within a family unless, again, the market has taken a sudden turn for the worse. The trick here is to do your homework and make sure sister and brother funds within the family have a good track record because you do not want to switch out of a tainted darling into a dog.

Some of the biggest mutual fund families like Benham Capital Management Group of Mountain View, California, have some of the better performing funds because they can afford top talent, and they know they can ill afford to have just one or two superstar funds to bring investors in the front door. They frequently offer several different variations on the government bond theme—all treasuries, a combination of treasuries and Ginnie and Fannie Maes, highly targeted funds that invest in zeros or treasuries.

Even if you feel you are too busy or too inexperienced to pick a U.S. Government mutual fund or feel uncomfortable *reading* red and green flags that may be waving, there are options. Certain investment management firms use only no-load mutual funds to invest their client assets. These firms monitor several thousand portfolio managers and decide, based on market conditions and client goals, when and where to switch funds. However, you do pay a fee for this service—one half to 1 percent of your total fund investment.

Finally, always look for an edge that will save you time, mistakes, and anxiety. If you like to take charge of your own money but still want a fixed income professional actually making the buy and sell decisions, Charles Schwab & Company, the nationwide discount brokerage firm, offers its Mutual Fund Marketplace. With a single phone call, this gives you access to 400 no-load and low-load stock and bond mutual funds.

In fact, you can really be creative with your investment strategies and be safe at the same time. Say you own a $25,000 bond paying 8 percent a year. You really don't want to sell the bond, but you seem to dribble away the semiannual coupon of $1,000. Or at the very least, it doesn't get the benefit of compounded interest. Burt Berry suggests keeping the bond and endorsing over the interest checks to an astutely managed, solidly performing no-load U.S. Government bond fund.

33

KEEPING AN OPEN MIND ABOUT CLOSED-END FUNDS

A mutual fund, by definition, usually is an open-end investment company. It continually sells and redeems shares, and you own shares of net asset. Again, that is the total market value of an investment company's shares—securities, cash, and any accrued earnings—minus its liabilities, and divided by the number of shares outstanding.

A mutual fund can also be a closed-end investment company. It issues a fixed number of shares and they are traded in the securities or stock market. They're usually bought and sold through stockbrokers. However, there are about 20 closed-end bond funds with treasury or government agency obligations in their portfolios. Some invest in foreign government obligations.

Closed-end bond funds offer the investor an edge. They pay dividends and often sell at a discount to their net asset value (although they can sell at a premium). You should rarely buy a closed-end bond fund when it's issued at 100 cents on the dollar because several months later it almost always sells at a discount of 5 to 10 percent from its net asset value.

Thomas J. Herzfeld, probably the savviest of all closed-end mutual fund investors and author of the *Encyclopedia of Closed-End Funds,* has a strategy of buying only the deepest discounted funds and watching interest rates and stock market behavior. "You have to see which way the market is moving in government bonds and the share prices for mutual funds that are not based on net asset value." That takes skill because the closed-end bond fund's share price in the stock market is not tied to the net asset value of the portfolio.

Hence, you can be right on an interest rate call and the portfolio's assets will expand, and wrong in the stock market because, for some unfathomable reason, the fund's per-share price can drop. Still, the wider the discount between the stock price and the NAV, the greater your potential for gain—especially in a closed-end U.S. Government bond fund.

Theoretically, you can be buying the most solid treasury obligations for as little as 85 cents on the dollar. But, frankly, to find closed-end bond fund shares trading 15 percent off the net asset value is rare.

Tagline: Closed-end fund investors are always looking for Judgment Day. That's the day closed-end funds go open-end and the discount immediately disappears, ensuring an automatic gain. The fact is, closed-ends don't open that often. But when they do, it's a windfall.

34

MUNI BOND MUTUAL FUNDS: LESS PAIN, MORE GAIN—MAYBE

There is no question that the tax-free yield from municipal bonds is tantalizing to any investors who want to reduce their annual tithe to Uncle Sam.

And when you consider that a municipal bond issued in the state where you live gives you two tax exemptions on the income—from federal and state tax—it's a wonder more investors don't buy only these so-called "double tax-frees."

But munis are not a slam dunk investment. Realistically, you need to commit at least $25,000 to individual munis to get significant tax-free return. What's more, although residents in large, financially sound states may have an array of state government obligation bonds to choose from, backed by the full faith and credit of the issuing state, investors elsewhere sometimes have to look to the riskier municipal revenue bonds to get that twin tax break.

Instead, you might want to consider the wisdom—and convenience—of a muni bond mutual fund, which you can buy into and sell out of anytime. There are an estimated 350 municipal bond funds in the marketplace today, and you can buy into a fund for as little as $250 and receive monthly cash dividends.

Mutual funds are especially attractive to muni bond investors because, depending on where you live, you can get the double tax-free benefits of what are called "single-state" mutual funds. That's where the fund portfolio holds only munis from a single state, thereby entitling you to the dual tax exemptions.

Muni bond funds have their share of fans. "We find the inefficiencies [illiquidity, large minimum costs] of the individual municipal bond market are so great investors are better off using the economies of scale of a professionally managed mutual fund," contends Ralph G. Norton III, editor and publisher of the Boston-headquartered *Muni Bond Fund Report*. Norton contends fund investors benefit from the diversification of a portfolio holding 600 to 800 different municipal bonds.

He makes another great case for muni bond mutual funds. "For the average investor, analyzing the credit-worthiness of a muni is difficult if not impossible unless they do it as a fulltime occupation or are willing to devote relatively significant resources to that task," says Norton. And he's right. Higher yields are often found in the riskier muni revenue bonds and it really takes a professional to size up the fiscal and operational soundness of the underlying project generating the revenue stream.

Muni bond mutual funds can cushion market risk and liquidity risk if interest rates rise and bond prices fall. "If the market starts to decline rapidly, holders of a small number of individual bonds get the worst deal of all trying to exit their positions with a reasonable price," Norton says.

However, Norton adds that shareholders in a mutual fund can "exit easily with normal options—redeeming their shares with a toll free phone call, switching their shares into another mutual fund, or just writing a check on their shares" to cash out.

In the meantime, fundholders who elect to stay invested and do not need the monthly income for living expenses can reinvest it a lot easier than an individual muni bondholder can. For instance, a fund yielding several hundred dollars a month doesn't generate enough cash to buy another municipal bond, but the income can be automatically reinvested to purchase additional shares. And, in a down market, falling fund prices mean each dividend dollar buys more shares.

35

THE DOWNSIDE OF MUNI BOND FUNDS

Municipal bond mutual funds also have their short-comings. Fund investors give up the fixed rate of interest they reap with an individual muni bond. The yield, while paid out as monthly dividend income, is an average of all munis in the portfolio.

"You really have to look at 'total return' and not just 'yield,' in evaluating a muni bond fund," stresses Sheldon Jacobs, editor and publisher of *The No-Load Fund Investor*. "You want dividends and capital appreciation." And like all government bond funds where returns rarely match stock fund returns, look for the highest performers with the lowest expenses.

Ralph Norton, publisher of the *Muni Bond Fund Report*, points to a second shortcoming. "There is no maturity date in a muni bond fund like there is with individual bonds, so, technically, there is no guarantee of a principal payback. It's essentially a perpetual investment." On the other hand, a bond fund investor can, theoretically, redeem at any time by cashing out.

A third shortcoming can be the mix of the bonds in the portfolio. In choosing a muni bond fund, read the prospectus to make sure the high tax-free yield isn't the result of overloading the fund with municipal revenue bonds that are issued by cities to finance public works projects. Since these bonds are repaid by revenues collected from the citizenry, they can default if the project is poorly run and doesn't generate enough cash. Obviously, these would carry higher risk, so the more generous payout could come with strings attached.

A fourth factor is that if you're in a high tax bracket, some municipals in a bond fund can trigger the Alternative Minimum Tax, which will actually add to your tax bill, notes Jacobs. The AMT, as it's called, may be triggered if you have enough tax preference deductions such as oil depletion allowance and accelerated depreciation as well as interest from a type of muni called a "private activity bond" issued after August 7, 1986.

How do you know if a fund portfolio holds bonds that will affect your AMT? You can use the fund's toll free number to call the portfolio manager and hope you get a straight answer. But there's always that worry because of bond turnover in the portfolio. Otherwise, you should consider a muni "unit trust" where the bonds do not change. Best advice here is to consult with your CPA.

The fifth thing to avoid is funds where the portfolio is stuffed with 30-year munis. Generally, with a flat or inverted yield curve, you do not get that much more income by going 15 to 30 years out compared to a portfolio comprised largely of intermediate maturities—seven to ten years. If you do have a positively sloped yield curve and then, as mentioned in Key 12, when the 30-year is yielding 1.5 percent more than seven- to ten-year maturities, it may be worth going into those longer bonds. But plan on staying in for a while rather than jumping out at the first jolt. And remember, a 30-year muni is every bit as volatile as a 30-year T-bond, so be watchful if the fund you're considering holds only long-term municipal bonds. These bonds will subject the fund to greater interest rate volatility and sharper swings in value.

Before you invest, research the *performance* and *risk* records of tax-exempt bond funds in references like the ninth edition of the American Association of Individual Investor's *Guide to No-Load Mutual Funds*. This publication ranked the Financial Income Fund as its top performing tax-exempt muni bond mutual fund from 1985 through 1989 with a 13.1 percent total annual return and a "below average" risk ranking.

That proves you can have it both ways—top performance and low risk. And if your muni bond fund is part of a family offering free exchanges, you can always switch into cash if you see an extended storm on the horizon.

In the meantime, if you can find a double tax-free mutual fund, where the portfolio holds only munis issued in the state where you reside, you could be home free, tax-free that is, and not pay a penny of taxes on the monthly income.

How tough are they to find? Any of the mutual fund directories cited in this book or the *Forbes* or *Barron's* annual mutual fund issues list them: Connecticut, New Jersey, California, Pennsylvania, Michigan, Ohio, and Massachusetts all have single-state mutual funds buying their municipal bonds. New York City residents may get the best deal of all. A New York tax-free muni bond gives investors a return that is exempt from federal, state, and city income taxes as well. It's not a painkiller for high-bracket taxpayers, but it can certainly help.

36

HARD TRUTHS AND SMART STRATEGIES FOR INFORMED INVESTORS

No matter where you put your money to work, remember this wisdom and adopt it as a fundamental belief: The informed investor who has skills to win has a better chance of being successful than the misinformed investor who needs luck to win.

Nowhere is this a harder truth than in the U.S. Government securities markets. The world of treasury bills, bonds, and notes and their fixed income siblings—agencies and munis—can no longer be categorized as simply "the bond market" where all investments act the same. Different sectors of the bond market perform independently, which is a new phenomenon.

For instance, we learned in the Persian Gulf crisis of 1990 that short-term interest rates fell because the market anticipated that the Federal Reserve would ease monetary policy to avoid recession, while long-term interest rates rose because the threat to the world oil supply triggered inflationary fears. Conventional wisdom always told us that all interest rates move in the same direction—but no longer.

These new phenomena demand that you explore hard truths and analyze time-and-market-tested strategies for informed investors.

The first, most fundamental step for investing in U.S. Government securities is to make a decision about interest rates. Will they go up? Will they go down? Will they stay put? What is the general trend?

If you've done your homework, read the periodicals and listened to the gurus, and you are still genuinely unsure, stay short-term. Buy three-month, six-month, or one-year T-bills and roll them over. You have liquidity, a yield comparable to money market mutual funds and a temporary floor if rates go down.

However, when you do form an opinion on interest rates—whether bullish (rates will drop, bond prices will rise) or bearish (rates will cimb, prices will fall)—you must then pick a maturity sector. The farther out you go on the maturity spectrum, the greater the price volatility, hence the higher the risk and the larger the reward. As we've said before, short and intermediate maturities (one to seven years) will react less dramatically, in terms of price fluctuations, than longer maturities—T-bonds with 10- to 30-year maturities.

After forming your opinion on rates—and feeling comfortable with them—your next strategic step is to set a stop loss. Informed investors are disciplined, know how much they can lose and when to admit they are wrong.

Of course, that's easy to say (or write) but very tough to practice. Humans, by nature, hate to admit they're wrong. They rationalize, blame, freeze—do anything but admit they've made the wrong decision. For investors, that can be financially fatal. And in the long bond market, where, if you're long, even the slightest interest rate move against you can send prices—and your principal—plunging, not admitting you've made a mistake can be a very costly lesson in arrogance or ignorance.

So, form an opinion on rates, pick a maturity and set your stop losses.

Now, don't assume I've taken a header over the edge when I state, "You'll make more money when you're wrong than when you're right." To this, I must add, "if you're disciplined."

Let's go back to human nature for a moment. Most investors not only can't admit they're wrong, but they can't help committing the cardinal sin—they think the market is wrong *and they're right*. So, they do the worst thing possible—they add to a losing position—and then they lose even more as the market continues to drop. If they're investing on leverage, they get a margin call for more cash. And when the pain becomes unbearable, human nature dictates that the investor sell out and vow never again to go back into the market.

What should you do when you've made a wrong decision? Admit it as soon as possible, sell out, and reverse your position; if you were bearish, lock in a bullish position or vice versa. It's a slap to your pride, ego, and finances to confess that you made a mistake. We all hate failures. But if you act fast enough, you can capitalize on the error while other investors either become paralyzed by their losses or sour on the market.

Let's take another seemingly illogical step. The best thing that can happen to you, believe it or not, is to lose money in your first forays into the treasury market. If you win right off the bat, you can become cocky and emotional and throw discipline out the window. Instead of setting stop losses on every position, you feel you have the Midas touch.

What's more, you tend to reward yourself on early victories by selling out and crowing. It may be difficult for a loser to admit defeat, but it's just as hard for winners to enjoy their success by letting the winnings run and adding more positions. The axiom to cut losses and stick with winners is another hard truth that really applies to the fast-moving treasury market.

Losing cleanses the soul. When you're in a losing trade, you can't think straight until you make that disciplined decision to cut the losses and the pain and reverse your position. Your investing is a business, and business owners discontinue or discount merchandise that doesn't move; they don't sit with it or bail out of the business. They hold a clearance sale and restock.

The same is true for investors. If you are going to do more than just hold to maturity and clip coupons, you must learn to be a professional loser before you can ever become a professional winner.

37

SOME FRANK FACTS ON TREASURIES: AN INSIDER'S VIEW

No book on investing would be complete without a look at what really happens behind the scenes. How does the system view—and treat—the customer? What are the hard truths investors never, ever hear? To get it firsthand and unvarnished, a broker with a major Wall Street firm was given total anonymity in exchange for a frank insider's report. His code name: Deep Trader. The words are his.

JG: Why don't retail stockbrokers sell treasuries as actively as stocks? Poor commissions?

DT: That was the situation until mid-1988. Brokerages paid us too little. Now the big wire houses pay decent PC [Production Credit or Commission].

JG: What commissions do retail investors pay?

DT: Say you buy 30-year treasuries. You can negotiate commissions but, generally, you, the client, may pay a point and a quarter—1¼ percent.

JG: How many bonds would a client have to buy?

DT: Minimum five bonds [$5,000], maybe ten [$10,000]. But even at retail, the more bonds the client buys, the better it gets.

JG: Do clients ask for the 30-year? Do they know maturities or do you have to sell them on it?

DT: Today the brokerage firm mentality is pushing, pushing, pushing, but we're running into constraints by the clients. They're extremely sensitive toward current yield. You can tell them forever, "I think rates are going to drop; buy bonds now and lock them in." They don't listen. Then a year later, when rates are down two points, they agree with you and want to scalp the last couple of basis points off you.

JG: Okay, let's put the system to a test. Say I want to buy 50,000 8¾s of May 2020. The ask price on Telerate is 102¹/₃₂ but the minimum is $1 million. What's your quote?

DT: 104³/₃₂ for 50,000 bond. Out of that, I get a 1⅝ credit [commission]. The trader takes ⅜. The firm takes two thirds of the 1⅝ and I get one third.

JG: So your price is two points over institutional prices. Is that your "suggested" price? Doesn't a client complain?

DT: Depends. If someone is going to buy 100 bonds [$100,000], I know he's sophisticated enough to look at the price and say "hey, what is this?" So I go back into our screen and change my price. I do that as an accommodation to a good client. So instead of a point and a half [commission], I'll take a half point.

JG: Does the client ever ask how much you make on that bond?

DT: Rarely. But if he asks, I'll tell him the truth. Do I think other people always tell the truth? Doubtful.

JG: So as a broker you don't always have to do what your firm screen tells you to do?

DT: No. We have direct phone links to our traders and I'll use them to get a little better price from the trader direct. You also know anything in the computer will have a little extra tacked on.

JG: What do you say to the trader?

DT: Actually, I'll call a liaison to the trader on our government desk, put in the order, and he'll say "What do you want on it?," meaning how much do I want to make on it. Right there is when I figure the commission so I can give the client a quote.

JG: Suppose a client is betting interest rates are going down and wants to buy treasuries on margin. Is he charged the same interest rate as he would for margining stocks?

DT: Yes. 10¼ percent.

JG: Yet the repo rate is 7¼ percent at this moment.

Why should customers pay the broker loan rate instead of the repurchase agreement rate normally used to leverage treasuries? After all, there is no credit risk on the treasuries and there is on stocks.

DT: Yes, it is ridiculous.

JG: Do most clients get pushed into zero treasuries because the commissions are higher?

DT: I don't think so. Commissions aren't that much higher, maybe a half point.

JG: That's already pretty large.

DT: Yes, well, the truth is most clients get pushed into [bond] funds because they're easy. Which funds? The new ones, the rookies [brokers] who may have sold widgets and don't do a lot of thinking on their own, may sell the firm's own funds. I've been in the business for a long, long time and I find the best performers.

JG: Do brokerages themselves really push treasuries.

DT: Yes. Lately, they've been coming out with papers [sales bulletins] weekly to make sure clients own bonds, buy treasuries, for the big picture. But most investors simply don't like treasuries. Whenever I recommend "buy a 10-year treasury," 95 percent of the time, they say "how much do I lose when I sell it?" They only think about never-ending inflation and holding to maturity. They don't realize you can sell it earlier, hopefully at a market profit.

JG: If treasuries are so tough to sell, why are Ginnie Maes easier?

DT: Because they're looking at yield. The broker calls the client and says "rates are going down so lock in a yield now. I've got short treasuries at 8¼." The client knows CDs are 8.40. A money fund is 8¼. But when the broker says he has a longer Ginnie Mae paying 9⅛ percent, increasing your yield almost 1 percent, he goes for it, even though the market risk is higher. That's the problem. The investor doesn't really understand market risk.

Indeed, understanding is the key. And the only way to really understand the treasury market is to find a smart, seasoned broker willing to work with you over the long haul. Once you locate that person, forge a relationship built on pillars of trust and truth. Ask the hard questions and settle for nothing less than a step-by-step explanation of any aspect of treasuries that confuse you. Then reward your broker with loyalty during good markets and bad, victories as well as defeats. Fortunes are not built overnight and neither are professional friendships.

Be patient, be persistent, and you will be profitable.

QUESTIONS AND ANSWERS

Q. I'm a physician with a pension plan and I'm not planning to retire for another ten years. Most of the assets are in a money market fund, but some of my other colleagues told me I should be in zero-coupon treasuries. What's the smartest strategy?

A. Without knowing your personal financial situation, goals, and needs, it is impossible to make a firm recommendation one way or the other. But, here are some "pro" and "con" guidelines. On the plus side, zeros allow you to pick your maturities and lock in a fixed rate of appreciation. Zero treasuries are safe and secure. So, when you actually retire and want to buy that camper or that outboard motorboat, you will have the cash.

On the negative side, if interest rates go up, you are locked in at a lower yield to maturity. And because the coupon has been stripped off, there is no income to reinvest at higher rates. Nevertheless, if you see higher rates on your horizon, a sounder, simpler strategy might be to invest in three-month treasury bills and roll them over when they mature. Then you can take advantage of higher yields, should that occur.

Q. I understand the Treasury issues a special class of savings bond that is tax free if the proceeds are used to pay for a child's college education. How does that work?

A. This is true, but it's not limited to children or college. Section 135 of the IRS Code says taxpayers can buy U.S. savings bonds to educate themselves, their spouse or their children and get up to 100 percent exclusion on their income tax. These are called "educational bonds" and may also be used to pay costs for a qualified trade school or technical training program.

But there are some catches. The tax exclusion is designed to benefit people who really need it. It phases out for married taxpayers earning between $60,000 and $90,000 and for single taxpayers with incomes between $40,000 and $50,000. Plus, to get the full exclusion, educational bonds cannot be purchased in the child's name; they must be bought in the name of the taxpayer.

On balance, if you qualify, savings bonds are a great way to build a tax-advantaged nest egg to pay for schooling. You can start small—a $50 bond costs only $25 in cash today—or buy as much as $30,000 in one year for a cash outlay of $15,000. And even if you don't use them for school, Series EE bonds have an array of nifty features.

Q. What is the most cost-effective way to buy Treasury bills?

A. Direct from Uncle Sam. You can buy T-bills from most banks and brokerage firms, but chances are you'll be charged a $25 to $60 administrative fee or commission, depending on whether it's a newly auctioned bill or one trading on the secondary market. However, all branches of the Federal Reserve or an office of the Bureau of Public Debt will sell you one at no cost.

Buying from the government is remarkably simple. You can buy newly auctioned treasuries through the mail by submitting a noncompetitive tender, thus automatically opening a Treasury Direct account. You receive your own account number for subsequent purchases and eliminate the middleman.

When you buy direct, though, all purchases must be accompanied by full payment—cashier's check, certified personal check, maturing treasury securities, or cash. Forget cash, though. You don't want to walk around with or mail the minimum $10,000 that a T-bill costs.

Q. I've been thinking of investing in government bond funds and was told to look into both open-end and closed-end funds. What's the difference between them?

A. An open-end fund is what most investors think of when you mention mutual funds. This type of fund creates new shares on demand as investors deposit money for purchases. Shares are bought at the net asset value and can be redeemed at any time for the prevailing market price, which can be higher or lower than the original purchase price. Open-end funds can be invested in stocks, bonds, money market instruments, or a combination of these, depending on the objectives of the fund, and can be classified as no-load (0 percent commission) to high load (8.5 percent commission). Research has shown no correlation between superior performance and high loads; I always recommend no-load funds so that all your money goes to work for you and is not siphoned off to pay a salesperson's commission. Closed-end funds issue a fixed number of shares and usually are bought and sold on a major exchange. These funds normally trade at a discount to their net asset value and do not continually issue new shares to meet the demand of deposits by investors. Closed-end funds, like stocks, with a set number of shares issued and tradable, respond more closely to the law of supply and demand and the desires of the marketplace than do open-end funds.

Q. I'm aware that T-bills, notes, and bonds have no credit risk since they are backed by the full faith and credit of the U.S. Government. What about government agency securities like Fannie Mae and Sallie Mae bonds?

A. The dozen or so agencies in the U.S. Government such as the Federal National Mortgage Association (Fannie Mae) or Student Loan Marketing Corp. (Sallie Mae) issue obligations backed by Uncle Sam, and the federal government, so far, has not allowed any agency to default on its debts (bond issues). However, these agencies do not carry the "full faith and credit" guarantee that makes them completely worry-free. In the past, agencies generally paid higher coupon rates to encourage investors to consider them instead of credit risk-free T-bills or T-bonds as a parking place for their cash. But agencies aren't the great deal they used to be, because the yields they generate are not that much higher than those from intermediate to long-term treasuries. And there is less liquidity in the agency market, with wider spreads between the bids and asks on these bonds. A final point to consider is that the income from *some* agencies is not exempt from state and local taxes; after paying these taxes on a higher coupon agency bond, you can end up netting less than if you had placed your money in a lower coupon T-bond. Be sure and check with your tax professional before committing your cash to buy an agency. And if you're looking at fund expenses, government bond funds that include agencies in their portfolios to raise their yields often charge a higher management fee than funds invested in all treasuries.

Q. I have $10,000 of "risk" money that I want to invest. Is this enough to put into the treasuries market and be able to reap significant rewards?

A. You might want to consider putting the multiplying power of leverage to work for you by buying or selling puts and calls on treasury futures. This is a very active and liquid market, but it is not for the conservative or novice investor; options on treasury futures are a form of gambling, and you need to have the knowledge and the stomach for it. And you must have a definite opinion about interest rates and their direction before you place your "bet." Buying calls reflects your thinking that bond prices will rise (interest rates will drop) before the expiration date on that option, and buying puts means you are convinced that bond prices will drop (as interest rates rise). Although there are no guarantees protecting your principal, if you bet wrong on interest rates, you are not hurt as badly with options on treasury futures as with buying the treasury future itself. You can choose not to exercise your option to buy the contract at its expiration date, thereby losing only the premium you put up initially to own that option. (Premiums can range from a few sixty-fourths up to $5,000 plus a flat commission fee for the transaction.) There is no ceiling on what you can "win." But remember, most investors lose money in the options market, so just like a casino, the odds are against your "beating the house."

Q. I am considering putting some of my money into a government bond fund. My broker tells me just to pick the one with the highest yield. Is it really that simple?

A. With government bond funds, it's tempting to look for the highest yield in order to increase monthly income. But remember, higher rewards are usually generated by exposing yourself to greater market risk. Not all government bond funds are rock solid and risk free. Read the prospectus for any fund you are considering to see if management stretches the parameters of fund policy to create the illusion of higher yields. Do they add longer maturities that suffer from larger price fluctuations and expose shareholders to greater market risk? Does the portfolio show a recent infusion of premium bonds with high coupons that generate high *current* yield but will actually dole out a loss when the bonds redeem at par? Make sure you ask for estimated "total return" to weed out these false expectations. And look for government agency bonds that may be boosting yields. Ginnie Maes, for instance, pay high yields because of their long maturities—which also means they're extremely volatile. And because these bonds are actually clusters of home mortgages, when interest rates drop and homeowners refinance, the Ginnie Maes are called and paid off, frequently at no profit to the holder. And if the prospectus mentions option-writing as part of the investment strategy, watch out for more "heads you lose, tails you lose or break even" scenarios. These can generate short-term gains that are not technically a true component of yield and can be damaging to long-term total return.

Q. I used to buy U.S. Government T-bonds, have them registered in my name and delivered to me. I recently made another purchase, and now my broker says I can't have them delivered to me. He says they've changed the system, and I shouldn't worry. What's going on? What happens if my brokerage goes under and I don't have a certificate to cash in at the Treasury?

A. Your broker is referring to what is known as "book entry" format. At the time of purchase, book-entry securities that are not represented by a certificate are registered in your name on the books of the U.S. Treasury. Many new issues of bonds fit this format because it cuts down on paperwork on the brokerage level and saves the investor from worry about lost or stolen certificates. You do not need to be concerned if your brokerage goes out of business since these bonds are guaranteed by the full faith and credit of the U.S. Government. The Treasury knows you as the owner of the bonds because of the entry made on their books; additional proof you should plan on submitting at the time of redeeming the bonds would include the confirmation you received at the time of purchase and a copy of your monthly statement from the brokerage showing positions held in your account.

Q. I study the financial pages of my newspaper every day for the prices given on treasury bonds and bills. Then, when I call my broker before the market opens to see about making a purchase, the quote he gives me is usually not the same as the one in the paper. Why is that?

A. The quotes you see in the financial pages are representative of prices paid on transactions of $1 million at the close of trading, or as close to 4 P.M. Eastern Time as possible, the prior business day. But remember, U.S. treasuries trade almost around the clock, around the world. So, by the time you're reading your morning paper and before trading even begins in New York, Chicago, or Los Angeles, Japan has transacted a full day of business and traders in London have been buying and selling for half their day. This activity by U.S. investors doing business with foreign brokers or by foreigners purchasing U.S. securities abroad sets the tone for the opening prices for buyers and sellers stateside.

Q. I'm confused about commissions when buying or selling treasuries through my broker. What should I expect to pay?

A. Two watchwords are in effect here: "ask" and "negotiate." There is no set schedule of commissions charged by all brokers on treasury transactions, so you need to ask the hard questions up front to determine how much of a bite potential brokers will be taking out of your investment dollar. They should not shy from walking you through the numbers of a transaction, step by step. If you're told that there is no commission on a particular trade, especially when dealing with new issues, be wary, and turn the tables. Ask what price you would be able to receive if you chose to sell that same security; the difference between that and the purchase price is the commission or markup the firm is factoring into the transaction. You should be no less careful when discussing mutual funds; ask what the load is on a fund that the broker recommends. Remember, loads are commissions paid by the fund to a broker or salesperson; the broker who is truly watching out for your best interests will recommend a no-load fund that meets your investment goals and does not merely generate commissions. And if you don't like what you hear, negotiate. You and your broker should be able to reach a compromise that is fair to both of you. If you show you are savvy, you can operate from a position of strength in building a foundation for a candid and profitable relationship.

GLOSSARY

Accrued interest Interest earned but not yet received on a bond between semiannual coupon dates. The buyer of the security pays the quoted dollar price plus accrued interest.

Arbitrage The art or, as sometimes is believed, the science by which one buys certain securities thought to be undervalued and simultaneously sells other securities. Most frequently used in government securities with yield curve transactions. Example: buying two-year T-notes and selling 30-year T-bonds in a belief the yield curve will steepen to a more positive slope (see Key 12).

Ask The price at which a security is offered by a seller.

Back up (1) When yields rise and prices fall, the market is said to back up. (2) When investors swap out of one security into another of shorter current maturity (for example, out of a five-year note into a two-year note), they are said to back up.

Basis point One one-hundredth of 1 percent (0.01 percent).

Bearer bond A bond that is not registered in the name of the owner and requires clipping of semiannual coupons in order for the paying agent or issuer to disburse the interest. Whoever presents the coupons receives that interest payment. More common is the registered bond where the owner receives semiannual interest through automatic electronic transfer from the issuer.

Bid The price a buyer is willing to pay for a security.

Book-entry securities The Treasury and federal agencies are moving to a book-entry system in which securities are not represented by engraved pieces of paper but are maintained in computerized records at the Fed in the names of member banks, which, in turn, keep records of the securities they own as well as those they are holding for customers.

Broker A person who brings buyers and sellers together for a commission paid by the initiator of the transaction or by both sides; a broker does not take a position.

Call An option that gives the holder the right but not the obligation to buy the underlying security at a specified price during a fixed time period.

Capital gain The sale price of a security minus the purchase price.

Carry The interest cost of financing securities held.

Commission A broker's fee for handling transactions for a client.

Coupon (1) The annual rate of interest on a bond's face value that a bond's issuer promises to pay the bondholder. (2) A certificate attached to a bearer bond evidencing interest due on a payment date.

Current yield Coupon payments on a security as a percentage of the security's market price.

Dealer In contrast to a broker, a person who acts as a principal in all transactions, buying and selling for his or her own account.

Discount bond A bond selling below its redemption value and generally paying interest below the current coupon rate.

Exercise price The price at which an option holder may buy or sell an underlying security; also called the striking price.

Expiration date The deadline when the holder of an option must exercise this option.

Federal funds Funds deposited by commercial banks at Federal Reserve banks, including funds in excess of bank reserve requirements; can be lent to other member banks on an overnight basis at the Federal funds rate.

Federal funds rate The rate of interest at which Fed funds are traded. This rate is generally pegged by the Federal Reserve through open-market operations.

Federal Reserve Board (FRB) A federal agency empowered by Congress to regulate credit in the United States. Its members are appointed by the president.

Federal Reserve requirements The percentage of its deposits that a commercial bank must set aside, determined by the Federal Reserve, in order to limit its potential credit-granting capability.

Federal Reserve System A system of Federal Reserve banks in the United States forming 12 districts under the control of the Federal Reserve Board. These banks regulate the extension of credit as well as other banking activities.

Form 1099-OID An IRS form listing taxable interest on zero-coupon securities or treasury bills. Required to be mailed to some holders of zeros.

Futures market A market in which contracts for future delivery of a commodity or a security are bought and sold.

Governments Negotiable U.S. Treasury securities.

Handle The whole-dollar price of a bid or offer. For example, if a security is quoted 98-16 bid and 98-17 offered, 98 is the handle. In quoting the market, traders would generally omit the handle and refer only to the spread 16-17, which represents 16 to 17 32nds.

Inflation A general rise in prices.

Leverage A strategy that offers the possibility of high return for a small cash outlay by requiring only partial payment for the security and financing the remainder of the purchase price.

Liquidity An asset that can be converted easily and rapidly into cash without a substantial loss of value. In the money market, a security is said to be liquid if the spread between bid and ask prices is narrow.

Load Difference between the net asset value and the price at which a mutual fund will sell shares. This is the commission paid to a broker or salesperson for selling the fund.

Long bonds Bonds with a long current maturity.

Margin The purchasing of securities, either stocks or bonds, on leverage. Generally, though, the interest rate charged for margining a security is higher than the repurchase or repo rate for leveraging bonds.

Market value The price at which a security is trading and could presumably be purchased or sold.

Maturity (date) The date on which a bond comes due; both principal and any accrued interest due are paid on this date.

Municipals Securities issued by state and local governments and their agencies.

Net asset value The actual value of a bond fund that charges no load.

Odd lot Less than a round lot.

Off-the-run issue In treasuries and agencies, an issue that is not included in dealer or broker runs. With bills and notes, normally only current issues are quoted.

Premium bond A bond selling above par.

Put An option that gives the holder the right but not the obligation to sell the underlying security at a specific price during a fixed time period.

Repurchase agreement (RP or REPO) An agreement between a holder of securities and an investor to repurchase securities at a fixed price on a fixed date. The security "buyer" in effect lends the "seller" money for the period of the agreement, and the terms of the agreement are structured to compensate the buyer for this. Dealers use RPs extensively to finance their positions. Exception: When the Fed is said to be doing RPs, it is lending money—that is, increasing bank reserves.

Reverse repurchase agreement Most typically, a repurchase agreement intiated by the lender of funds. Reverses are used by dealers to borrow securities they have shorted. Exception: When the Fed is said to be doing reverses, it is borrowing money—that is, absorbing reserves.

Round lot In the money market, round lot refers to the minimum amount for which dealers' quotes are good. This is usually $1 million in notes and bonds and $5 million in bills.

Savings bond A bond issued through the U.S. Government at a discount and in face values from $50 to $10,000. The interest is exempt from state and local taxes, and, if elected, no federal tax comes due until the bond is redeemed.

Settlement date The date on which a trade is cleared by delivery of securities against funds. Normally, government securities are settled on the next business day.

Short sale The sale of securities not owned by the seller in the expectation that the price of these securities will fall or as part of an arbitrage. A short sale must eventually be covered by a purchase of the securities sold.

Trade date The date on which a transaction is initiated. The settlement date may be the trade date or a later date.

Treasury bill A federal obligation issued in denominations of $10,000 to $1 million with a maturity date usually of three months to one year. It is fully marketable at a discount from face value (which determines the interest rate).

Treasury bond A federal obligation issued in denominations of $500 to $1 million with maturities ranging from five to 35 years, carrying a fixed interest rate and issued, quoted, and traded as a percentage of its face value.

Treasury note A federal obligation issued in denominations of $1,000 to $500 million for maturities of one to ten years, carrying a fixed rate of interest.

Yield curve A graph showing the relationship at a given point in time between yield and current maturity for securities that all expose the investor to the same credit risk. Yield curves are typically drawn by using yields on governments of various maturities.

Yield to maturity The rate of return yielded by a debt security held to maturity when both interest payments and the investor's capital gain or loss on the security are taken into account.

Zero-coupon bonds Bonds that make no semiannual interest payments and are sold at a deep discount from face value; created when a brokerage strips the coupons off a T-bond and sells the corpus (principal) separately from the coupons. Examples of government zeros are CATS, STRIPS, and TIGRS.

APPENDIX

THE FEDERAL RESERVE
AND ITS BRANCHES

In addition to the office of the Board of Governors of the Federal Reserve System in Washington, D.C., there are twelve main branches of the Fed and 22 local offices. Each one has a Public Affairs Office that can supply investors with a wealth of free pamphlets, charts, statistics, special publications, and audiovisual materials about the Fed system, monetary policy, financial markets and the economy. Their addresses and phone numbers are listed below.

Board of Governors of the Federal Reserve System
Publications Services
MS-138
Washington, DC 20551
(202) 452-3244

Federal Reserve Bank of Atlanta
Public Information Department
104 Marietta Street NW
Atlanta, GA 30303-2713
(404) 521-8788

Birmingham Branch   (205) 731-8500
Jacksonville Branch   (904) 632-1000
Miami Branch   (305) 591-2065
Nashville Branch   (615) 251-7100
New Orleans Branch   (504) 586-1505

Federal Reserve Bank of Boston
Public Services Department
P.O. Box 2076
Boston, MA 02106-2076
(617) 973-3459

Federal Reserve Bank of Chicago
Public Information Center
230 South LaSalle Street
P.O. Box 834
Chicago, IL 60690
(312) 322-5111

Detroit Branch (313) 961-6880

Federal Reserve Bank of Cleveland
Public Affairs Department
P.O. Box 6387
Cleveland, OH 44101-1387
(216) 579-3079

Cincinnati Branch (513) 721-4787
Pittsburgh Branch (412) 261-7800

Federal Reserve Bank of Dallas
Public Affairs Department
Station K
Dallas, TX 75222
(214) 651-6289/6266

Federal Reserve Bank of Kansas City
Public Affairs Department
925 Grand Avenue
Kansas City, MO 64198
(816) 881-2402

Denver Branch	(303) 572-2300
Oklahoma City Branch	(405) 270-8400
Omaha Branch	(402) 221-5500

Federal Reserve Bank of Minneapolis
Public Affairs
250 Marquette Avenue
Minneapolis, MN 55480
(612) 340-2446

Helena Branch (406) 442-3860

Federal Reserve Bank of New York
Public Information Department
33 Liberty Street
New York, NY 10045
(212) 720-6134
(Also maintains a directory, *Public Information Materials,* which is updated every two years and lists many of the materials offered by the other branches of the Fed, organized by subject area. A supplement is published in alternate years.)

Buffalo Branch (716) 849-5000

Federal Reserve Bank of Philadephia
Public Information Department
P.O. Box 66
Philadephia, PA 19105
(215) 574-6115
(Also publishes a biannual index, *The Fed in Print,* which lists many of the special publications of the Reserve Banks and the Board of Governors.)

Federal Reserve Bank of Richmond
Public Services Department
P.O. Box 27622
Richmond, VA 23261
(804) 697-8109

Baltimore Branch	(301) 576-3300
Charlotte Branch	(704) 358-2100

Federal Reserve Bank of St. Louis
Public Information Office
P.O. Box 442
St. Louis, MO 63166
(314) 444-8444, ext. 545

Little Rock Branch	(501) 372-5451
Louisville Branch	(502) 568-9200
Memphis Branch	(901) 523-7171

Federal Reserve Bank of San Francisco
Public Information Department
P.O. Box 7702
San Francisco, CA 94120
(415) 974-2163

Los Angeles Branch	(213) 683-2903
Portland Branch	(503) 221-5900
Salt Lake City Branch	(801) 322-7926
Seattle Branch	(206) 343-3638

BROADCAST RESOURCES

The following television and radio business programs as well as cassette tape services provide news, analysis, and opinion on the U.S. Government bond market plus domestic and world economic events affecting interest rate movements.

Television

Cable News Network (CNN)

Business Morning	with Stuart Varney (Mon/Fri)
Business Day	with Stuart Varney (Mon/Fri)
Moneyline	with Lou Dobbs (Mon/Fri)
Your Money	with Stuart Varney (Sat)
Moneyweek	with Lou Dobbs (Weekends)
Inside Business	with Myron Kandel (Sun)

Public Broadcasting Service (PBS)

| *Wall Street Week* | with Louis Rukeyser (Fri) |
| *Nightly Business Report* | with Paul Kangas (Mon/Fri) |

CNBC (24-hour cable news programming)
    Smart Money   with Ken and Daria Dolans (Mon/Fri)

Financial News Network (FNN) (24 hour cable network)

World Business Report	(Mon/Fri)
Market Preview	(Mon/Fri)
IRS Tax Beat	*(Mon/Fri)*
Your Financial Future	(Mon/Fri)
Investor's Daily Business	with William O'Neil
Show	(Mon)
Moneytalk	(Mon/Fri)
Marketwatch	(Mon/Fri)
Marketwrap	(Mon/Fri)

ESPN (Cable Television network)
    Nation's Business Today   (Mon/Fri)
NBC News with Alan
  Abelson, editor of
  Barron's, offers daily
  market analysis on
  Early Today Show   (Mon/Fri)

Radio

CNN Radio Network (350 stations nationwide)
  Seven business reports daily

  Business Morning   with Stuart Varney

Audiotape Business and Financial News

Investment Insights   with Paul Houston
(800-334-5771)
Investor's Hotline   with Joe Bradley
(800-345-8112)

NEWSLETTERS

Although lengthy, the following is only a partial list of the sources of information available by subscription or membership. Newsletters are listed alphabetically, and although we have divided them into three categories—

fundamentals, technical, and mutual fund—we have made no attempt to rank them. If a particular publication interests you, I would suggest you write to their office and request a sample copy. If you happen to run across an outstanding source of information for the debt market investor that is not included in this list, drop me a note and I'll add that newsletter to the next edition of this book.

Fundamentals

AAII Journal (Nonprofit)
American Association of
  Individual Investors
625 North Michigan
  Avenue
Chicago, IL 60611

A. Gary Shilling &
  Company, Inc.
Economic Consultants
  and Investment
  Strategists
500 Morris Ave.
Springfield, NJ 07081

Bank Credit Analyst
BCA Publications
3463 Peel Street
Montreal, Quebec,
  Canada H3A 1W7

Bank Rate Monitor
Box 088888
North Palm Beach, FL
  33408-8888

*Blue Chip Economic
  Indicators*
Capital Publications, Inc.
1101 King Street

P.O. Box 1454
Alexandria, VA 22313-
  2054

Bond Buyer's Alert
KCI Communication
1101 King Street, Suite
  400
Alexandria, VA 22314

Bondweek
488 Madison Avenue,
  14th Floor
New York, NY 10022

The Business Picture
Gilman Research
  Company
P.O. Box 20567
Oakland, CA 94620

*California Municipal
  Bond Advisor*
Arenas Building, Suite 25
P.O. Box 1962
Palm Springs, CA 92263

*Defaulted Bonds
  Newsletter* (Nonprofit)

Bond Investors
  Association, Inc.
P.O. Box 4427
Miami, FL 33014-2400

*Dessauer's Journal of
  Financial Markets*
P.O. Box 1718
Orleans, MA 02653

The Financial Economist
Strategic Investment
  Services
1325 Morris Drive, Suite
  201
Wayne, PA 19087

*Grant's Interest Rate
  Monitor*
233 Broadway, Suite 1216
New York, NY 10279

Griggs & Santow Report
Griggs & Santow, Inc.
One World Trade Center,
  Suite 2509
New York, NY 10048

*High Frequency
  Economics*
584 Broadway
New York, NY 10012

Industry Forecast
Levy Economic Forecasts
Box 26
Chappaqua, NY 10514

Investor's Hotline (tape
  service)

10616 Beaver Dam Road
Hunt Valley, MD 21030

The Main Street Journal
Claremont Economics
  Institute
143 North Harvard
  Avenue, Suite E
Claremont, CA 91711

Market Trim Tabs
P.O. Box 2949
Santa Rosa, CA 95405

Money-Forecast Letter
Financial Research
  Center, Inc.
7 October Hill Road
Holliston, MA 01746

*Nielsen's International
  Investment Letter*
P.O. Box 7532
Olympia, WA 98507

100 Highest Yields
P.O. Box 088888
North Palm Beach, FL
  33408-8888

*Perception for the
  Professional*
The Leuthold Group
700 Butler Square
100 North 6th Street
Minneapolis, MN 55403

Quantum
1272 West Pender Street

Vancouver, BC Canada
V6E 2S8

*Washington Bond &
Money Market Report*
1545 New York Avenue
NE
Washington, DC 20002

*Wells Fargo Economic
Monitor*
Wells Fargo Bank/
Economics 0188-057
111 Sutter Street
San Francisco, CA 94163

Technical Information

Bond Market Strategy
Ned Davis Research, Inc.
5600 Glenridge Drive,
#210
Atlanta, GA 30342

*Bridgewater Daily
Observations*
Bridgewater Associates
372 Danbury Road
Wilton, CT 06897

*Bullish Consensus and
Commodity Futures*
Hadady Corporation, Inc.
1111 S. Arroyo Parkway,
Suite 410
P.O. Box 90490
Pasadena, CA 91109-0490

*Commodity Traders
Consumer Report*
1731 Howe Avenue, Suite
149
Sacramento, CA 95825

FullerMoney
Chart Analysis, Ltd.
7 Swallow Street
London, England W1R
7HD

*Futures Hotline/Bond
Fund Timer*
Davis/Zweig Futures, Inc.
P.O. Box 360
Bellmore, NY 11710

Hulbert Financial Digest
316 Commerce Street
Alexandria, VA 22314

Interest Rate Report
2260 Cahuenga
Boulevard, Suite 305
Los Angeles, CA 90068

Investor's Digest (tape
service)
3471 North Federal
Highway
Fort Lauderdale, FL
33306

Mamis Guide
Gordon Capital, Inc.
767 Fifth Avenue, 50th
Floor
New York, NY 10153-
0101

Market Beat, Inc.
1436 Granada
Ann Arbor, MI 48103

MBH Weekly Commodity
  Letter
MBH Commodity
  Advisors, Inc.
Box 353
Winnetka, IL 60093

Option Advisor
P.O. Box 46709
Cincinnati, OH 45245

Personal Finance
KCI Communications
1101 King Street, Suite
  400
Alexandria, VA 22314-
  2980

Peter Eliades'
  Stockmarket Cycles
  Interest Rate Report
2260 Cahuenga
  Boulevard, Suite 305
Los Angeles, CA 90068

Pring Market Review
International Institute for
  Economic Research
P.O. Box 329
Washington Depot, CT
  06794

Timer Digest
Timer Digest Publishing
P.O. Box 1688
Greenwich, CT 06836-
  1688

Volume Reversal Survey
P.O. Box 1451
Sedona, AZ 86336

Mutual Fund Information

Closed-End Fund Digest
1280 Coast Village Circle,
  Suite C
Santa Barbara, CA 93108

Donoghue's Money Fund
  Report
360 Woodland Street
P.O. Box 6640
Holliston, MA 01746

Donoghue's Moneyletter
360 Woodland Street
P.O. Box 6640
Holliston, MA 01746

Fidelity Monitor
Fidelity Investors, Inc.
P.O. Box 1294
Rocklin, CA 95677-7294

Global Fund Timer
P.O. Box 77330
Baton Route, LA 70879

Income & Safety
3471 North Federal
  Highway
Fort Lauderdale, FL
  33306

Investment Company Institute
1600 M Street NW
Washington, DC 20036

Investor's Guide to Closed-End Funds
Thomas J. Herzfeld
Advisors, Inc.
P.O. Box 161465
Miami, FL 33116

Lynch Municipal Bond Advisory
P.O. Box 1086
Lenox Hill Station
New York, NY 10021

Muni Bond Fund Report
Box 2179
Huntington Beach, CA 92647

Mutual Fund Forecaster
3471 North Federal Highway
Fort Lauderdale, FL 33306

Mutual Fund Guide
Fidelity Investments
82 Devonshire Street, Dept. R25A
Boston, MA 02109

The Mutual Fund Letter
Investment Information Services, Inc
680 North Lake Shore Drive, Tower Suite 2038
Chicago, IL 60611

Mutual Fund News Service
Green Financial Communications, Inc.
P.O. Box 937
Bodega Bay, CA 94923-0937

Mutual Fund Performance Report
Morningstar, Inc.
53 West Jackson Boulevard
Chicago, IL 60604

Mutual Fund Sourcebook
53 W. Jackson Boulevard
Chicago, IL 60604

Mutual Fund Values
53 West Jackson Boulevard
Chicago, IL 60604

No-Load Fund Investor
P.O. Box 283
Hastings-on-Hudson, NY 10706

NoLoad Fund X
DAL Investment Company
235 Montgomery Street
San Francisco, CA 94104

No-Load Mutual Fund
    Selections & Timing
    Newsletter
1120 Empire Central
    Place, Suite 315
Dallas, TX 75247

Paul Merriman's Fund
    Exchange
Paul A. Merriman &
    Associates, Inc.
1200 Westlake Avenue N
Seattle, WA 98109-3530

No-Load Portfolios
Portfolio Strategies, Inc.
527 Hotel Plaza
Boulder City, NV 89005

The Scott Letter: Closed-
    End Fund Report
Box 17800
Richmond, VA 23226

BOOKS

Reference books are useful for all investors, from the novice to the market veteran. Here is but a sampling of currently available publications dealing with aspects of the government bond market. New books are released on a regular schedule by most of the publishing houses named below. You can write to them to receive periodic mailings listing new books scheduled to be published.

American Association of Individual Investors. *The Individual Investor's Guide to Investment Publications.* International Publishing Corp., 1989.

―――. *The Individual Investor's Guide to No-Load Mutual Funds,* 9th ed. International Publishing Corp., 1990.

Berlin, Howard. *Dow Jones–Irwin Guide to Buying and Selling Treasury Securities.* Dow Jones–Irwin, 1988.

―――. *Handbook of Financial Market Indexes, Averages and Indicators.* Dow Jones–Irwin, 1990.

Burroughs, Eugene B. *Investment Terminology.* International Foundation of Employee Benefit Plans, 1984.

Capiello, Frank. *Complete Guide to Closed-End Funds.* International Publishing Corp., 1989.

Conrad, Roger. *Best Bond Plays of the 1990s.* KCI Communications, 1989.

Cook, Timothy Q. and Timothy Rowe. *Instruments of the Money Market,* 6th ed. Federal Reserve Bank of Richmond, 1988.

Donoghue, William. *Donoghue's Mutual Funds Almanac,* 21st ed. Donoghue Organization, 1990.

Douglas, Livingston G. *Bond Risk Analysis: A Guide to Duration and Convexity*. New York Institute of Finance, 1990.

———. *Yield Curve Analysis*. New York Institute of Finance, 1988.

Downes, John and Jordan Elliot Goodman. *Dictionary of Finance and Investment Terms,* 2nd ed. Barron's Educational Series, 1991.

———. *Barron's Finance and Investment Handbook,* 3d ed. Barron's Educational Series, 1990.

Fabozzi, Frank J. *The Handbook of Treasury Securities: Trading and Portfolio Strategies*. Probus Publishing Co., 1987.

Fabozzi, Frank J. and Irving M. Pollack. *The Handbook of Fixed Income Securities*. Dow Jones–Irwin, 1983.

The Investment Company Institute's Guide to Mutual Funds. Investment Company Institute, 1989.

Jacobs, Sheldon. *The Handbook for No-Load Fund Investors*. No-Load Fund Investor, 1989.

Jones, David M. *Fed Watching and Interest Rate Projections: A Practical Guide*. New York Institute of Finance, 1989.

United States Treasuries: Basic Information. Federal Reserve Bank of Dallas, 1984.

PRIMARY DEALERS

The following primary dealers in government securities all publish market research and economic commentary. If you wish to be placed on their mailing list for updates, contact the office of the chief economist.

Bank of America NT & SA
335 Madison Avenue
New York, NY 10017

Barclays de Zoete Wedd
Securities, Inc.
75 Wall Street
New York, NY 10265

Bear, Stearns &
Company, Inc.
245 Park Avenue
New York, NY 10167

BNY Securities, Inc.
48 Wall Street, 13th Floor
New York, NY 10286

BT Securities Corporation
One Bankers Trust Plaza
New York, NY 10006

Carroll McEntee &
McGinley, Inc.
40 Wall Street
New York, NY 10005

Chase Securities, Inc.
717 Fifth Avenue
New York, NY 10022

Chemical Securities, Inc.
277 Park Avenue, 10th
Floor
New York, NY 10172

Citicorp Securities
Markets, Inc.

55 Water Street, 43rd
Floor
New York, NY 10043

Continental Bank,
National Association
231 South LaSalle Street
Chicago, IL 60697

CRT Government
Securities, Ltd.
7 Hanover Square
New York, NY 10004

Daiwa Securities
America, Inc.
One World Financial
Center
200 Liberty Street
New York, NY 10281

Dean Witter Reynolds,
Inc.
2 World Trade Center
New York, NY 10048

Dillon, Read &
Company, Inc.
535 Madison Avenue
New York, NY 10022

Discount Corporation of
New York
58 Pine Street
New York, NY 10005

Donaldson, Lufkin &
Jenrette Securities
Corporation

140 Broadway
New York, NY 10005

The First Boston
   Corporation
55 East 52nd Street
Park Avenue Plaza
New York, NY 10055

First Chicago Capital
   Markets, Inc.
One First National Plaza,
   Suite 0463
Chicago, IL 60670

Fuji Securities, Inc.
140 South Dearborn
   Street
Chicago, IL 60603

Goldman, Sachs &
   Company
85 Broad Street
New York, NY 10004

Greenwich Capital
   Markets, Inc.
600 Steamboat Road
Greenwich, CT 06830

Harris Government
   Securities, Inc.
45 Broadway, 19th Floor
   Atrium
New York, NY 10006

Kidder, Peabody &
   Company, Inc.
10 Hanover Square
New York, NY 10005

Aubrey G. Lanston &
   Company, Inc.
20 Broad Street
New York, NY 10005

Manufacturers Hanover
   Securities Corporation
270 Park Avenue
New York, NY 10017

Merrill Lynch
   Government Securities,
   Inc.
250 Vesey Street
World Financial Center,
   North Tower
New York, NY 10281

J.P. Morgan Securities,
   Inc.
23 Wall Street
New York, NY 10015

Morgan Stanley &
   Company, Inc.
1251 Avenue of the
   Americas
New York, NY 10020

Nikko Securities
   Company International,
   Inc.
200 Liberty Street
New York, NY 10281

Nomura Securities
   International, Inc.
180 Maiden Lane, 31st
   Floor
New York, NY 10038

Paine Webber, Inc.
1285 Ave. of the
Americas
New York, NY 10019

Prudential-Bache
Securities, Inc.
One Seaport Plaza
New York, NY 10292

Salomon Brothers, Inc.
One New York Plaza
New York, NY 10004

Sanwa-BGK Securities
Co., L.P.
599 Lexington Avenue
New York, NY 10022

Security Pacific National
Bank
333 South Hope Street
Los Angeles, CA 90009

Shearson Lehman Hutton
Government Securities,
Inc.
American Express Tower
World Financial Center
New York, NY 10285

Smith Barney, Harris
Upham & Company,
Inc.
1345 Avenue of the
Americas
New York, NY 10105

SBC Government
Securities, Inc.
222 Broadway
Box 395, Church Street
Station
New York, NY 10008

UBS Securities, Inc.
299 Park Avenue
New York, NY 10171

S.G. Warbug &
Company, Inc.
787 Seventh Avenue
Equitable Tower, 26th
Floor
New York, NY 10019

Yamaichi International
(America), Inc.
Two World Trade Center
New York, NY 10048

INDEX

135